Ellen G. White's Classic *Steps to Christ* Adapted for Children

DAVID ASKS WHY

Ellen G. White's
Classic *Steps to Christ*
Adapted for Children

DAVID ASKS WHY

MELANIE TROXELL

Pacific Press® Publishing Association

Nampa, Idaho
Oshawa, Ontario, Canada
www.pacificpress.com

Design by Steve Lanto
Design resources from dreamstime.com and iStockphoto.com

Copyright © 2009 by Pacific Press® Publishing Association
Printed in the United States of America
All rights reserved

Additional copies of this book are available by calling toll-free 1-800-765-6955 or by visiting www.adventistbookcenter.com.

Bible texts are paraphrased by the author. The author's commentary is based on *Steps to Christ* by Ellen G. White.

Library of Congress Cataloging-in-Publication Data:

Troxell, Melanie, 1977-
David asks why : Ellen G. White's classic Steps to Christ adapted to children / Melanie Troxell.
p. cm.
ISBN-13: 978-0-8163-2254-1 (pbk.)
ISBN-10: 0-8163-2254-6 (pbk.)
1. Salvation—Seventh-day Adventists—Juvenile literature. 2. Christian life—Seventh-day Adventist authors—Juvenile literature. 3. Seventh-day Adventists—Doctrines—Juvenile literature. 4. White, Ellen Gould Harmon, 1827–1915. Steps to Christ—Juvenile literature. I. Title.
BT751.3.T76 2009
248.2'4—dc22

2009023718

09 10 11 12 13 • 5 4 3 2 1

Dedication

To my boys, Jonathan, Christian, and Noah, and to every other little child who wants to know Jesus better!

Acknowledgments

I want to say thank you to my husband, Mike, for being my best friend and my fan club.

I want to say thanks especially to my mom for watching my kids during my sickness and helping me complete this book, and for her constant assistance with ideas and editing.

Contents

A Brand-New Heart

David crept quietly into the room and along the side of the big bed.

"Rrrrrr!" he screamed. This was his most convincing lion's roar. He flew through the air and crashed onto the pile of pillows that his mother was sitting against. She wrinkled up her nose and grabbed his head, stuffing his face into a pillow. Then she grabbed him up in a hugful of tickles.

"Mommy, are you *done* on the computer yet? I want to go outside!"

He had asked many times already, but Mrs. Peppers was not feeling well. The weather was too cold for her to get excited about a walk in the woods.

She sighed and then smiled, setting her computer and books aside.

"OK, let me get your sister up, and then we'll get ready to go."

After bundling up in warm clothes, David, Christy, and their mother headed for the woods. Several times they stopped to notice interesting sticks and strange-looking rocks. Christy found a little yellow flower. She especially liked the bugs on the trail. She stopped and watched a fat beetle scurrying along the path. Christy poked it with a weed. When the beetle turned around to fight, she laughed.

A while later, they came back inside the house. Mrs. Peppers began to fix a warm drink for the boy and girl. While they waited, David discovered something he had not seen before. He saw a stack of computer paper in a folder on the kitchen table.

"What is in there?" he asked.

Mrs. Peppers smiled and set the warm drinks in front of her two children. She sat down and opened the folder. "Listen," she said. "I'll read it to you."

Do you like to go outside? The beautiful things God has made show you just how much He loves you. The Bible is full of stories to tell you of His love.

Think about the many things God has made. He created our world with everything you need to make you happy and healthy. The sunshine and the rain, the trees and water and grass are all special presents that God has given to you! God loves to help you grow and be happy.

King David says, "We are filled with hope and trust in God. We know that He will give us the food that we need. We are sure that He will give us our desires" (Psalm 145:15, 16).

When God made Adam and Eve, people were always good and happy; and the beautiful world was perfect, with no rottenness or death. But now there are many bad things in our world. Plants and animals and people get old and die. But even though people are hurting, we can still see God's love around us.

Sometimes our lives are hard. Sometimes we get hurt, and when we work, we get tired. But these troubles can help us learn and grow. Sometimes things go wrong, of course, but if we will just go outside, we will see all sorts of living things in nature that give us hope and comfort. We will find lovely roses among the thorns, and flowers among the prickles.

You can see God's love in the tiny opening flower buds and in every little piece of grass. The birds fill the air with their pretty songs, and the flowers smell delicious. The trees make the world seem alive with bright green. All of these teach us that God is a tender, loving Father, and He loves to make us happy.

What Did Jesus Do?

All week long, David had been looking forward to going to the Allstons' house for prayer meeting. He had always liked Mr. and Mrs. Allston because they paid attention to him and talked to him as though he understood. He had a hard time sitting through all the talking. But he enjoyed the popcorn and juice, and he tried to listen.

David had heard the grown-ups talking about why Jesus came to earth, and he didn't understand it. On the way home, he asked, "Dad, why *did* Jesus come here? I don't think I would have liked to leave heaven and my family very much."

To help him understand, Mr. Peppers pulled the folder of papers out of Mrs. Peppers's bag and began to read.

The Bible tells us all about God. That's where He tells us about His love and kindness. Many years ago, Moses asked God to show him His glory. God told him about just how good He is. People talk a lot about God's glory, but what does that mean? God's glory is His goodness.

The Lord told Moses, "I am kind, and I love to give you gifts that you don't deserve. I am patient with you and full of goodness. I cannot lie. I am kind to everyone, and I love to forgive sins" (Exodus 34:6, 7).

DAVID ASKS WHY

God uses many wonderful gifts to teach us to love Him. Do you love your family? Do you love your friends? This love is one way that God teaches us how great He is!

Even though God has shown us how much He loves us in many ways, some people still don't understand that He loves them. Satan has made people afraid of God. He has made people think God is mean and bad. The people think that God wants to hurt us and take everything good away from us. Satan has made people think that God likes it when people make a mess of things and that He wants to punish them. But that is not true! To teach us how much He really loves us, God sent His Son, Jesus, to earth to be born as a baby. Jesus came down from heaven to show us what God is like.

Have you ever seen God? The Bible says that no one has seen Him except for Jesus (John 1:18; Matthew 11:27). Would you like to see God, your Father in heaven? When we learn about Jesus, we are seeing a lovely picture of God (John 14:8, 9).

Why did Jesus come to earth? He came to preach good news to poor, sad people. He came to make sad hearts happy and to free people from their sinful habits (Luke 4:18). He did good things for everyone He met and healed many sick people. In everything He did, Jesus was loving and kind. He loves people very much.

Jesus became a little child, and then a man, just so He could understand what we need. Even poor people and shy people were never afraid of Him. Little children loved Jesus—they loved to sit on His lap and look into His friendly eyes.

God Loves Me

Jesus always told the truth, but was always kind when He did it. Jesus was thoughtful as He spoke to people and was never, ever rude. He didn't like the bad things people did, but He loved the people, so He taught them not to do those bad things. And He taught them to believe in their Father in heaven.

Sometimes Jesus cried when people did evil deeds because He felt pity for them. He was not afraid to say, very clearly, what a sin is. People were often mean to Him and didn't believe in Him, but He still loved them. He was never selfish, and He cared about every person on earth. He wanted to help everyone go to heaven.

Jesus Instead of Me

The Peppers family had spent a wonderful afternoon at the state park. They had not visited the park for a long time, and everyone was having fun. They had climbed to the top of the highest point in the park and felt the wind almost blow them off the little mountain.

The way back down seemed rougher and steeper, and the thorns seemed to scratch everyone when they weren't looking. Mr. Peppers was holding David's and Christy's hands to keep them steady. Suddenly, Christy noticed a big rock, and she pulled away to climb it. Her father hurried over just in time to catch her by the foot as she started to slide down over the six-foot drop on the other side of the rock.

Christy was scared, but she had not seen the real danger she was in. David and his parents knew

how scary it really was. At the bottom of the rock was a pile of stones and thorns that could have hurt Christy badly. David's heart was pounding in his ears. He loved his little sister and felt glad that she was safe. While his mother was checking Christy over, his father was holding up his left hand, looking at it carefully. David scooted over the steep trail on his bottom to where his father was squatting and asked to see his hand.

"Oh! It's bleeding! Are you OK, Daddy?"

"I'm OK. I'm just glad Christy is all right. That was really scary!"

That evening at home, Mrs. Peppers called everyone to come for a story. She pulled out the folder full of papers and began to read.

Jesus was kind and good, and so is God, His Father. Jesus had a hard life and died a very sad death, but He did it all so we wouldn't have to die. He wants us to be happy with Him in heaven forever. That is why Jesus came to this earth and became a human being like us.

Jesus lived and suffered and died to save you and me from sin and death. He took away our sadness so we could be happy forever. God let His precious Son, Jesus, come from a wonderful, glorious home in heaven down to our sad, dark earth. There is no death in heaven, but Jesus came to earth where sin and death are all around. He was willing to be insulted and hated for our sake. Because He was punished for our sin and died, we can be free and holy (Isaiah 53:5).

Think about the time when Jesus was alone in the desert. Think about Him praying tenderly for you in the Garden of Gethsemane. Think about Him dying on the cross! Jesus was perfect, and He took our sins on Himself. Jesus and His Father had been one, and when He died on the cross, Jesus felt very lonely. His heart hurt terribly, and before He died, He cried out, "My God, why have You left Me all alone?" (Matthew 27:46).

God Loves Me

Sin is such a bad thing—it hurts God very much. Because of sin, Jesus felt very far from God, His Father. The awfulness of sin and the loneliness for His Father killed Jesus, because it broke His heart.

Did Jesus die so that God would begin to love you? No, no! God has always loved you. He showed us how much He loved us by giving Jesus to die for us (John 3:16). While Jesus was hurting so much on the cross, God the Father was hurting too. Sin is always bad, and it must always be punished. God took the punishment for us by allowing Jesus to die instead of us.

God loves you so much that His love for Jesus grew even greater when Jesus died to save you (John 10:17). When someone sins, there must be a punishment. And so Jesus made things right and fair by letting Himself be punished for our sins.

Only Someone who knew God very well could save us from having to die for our own sins. Well, Jesus *is* God, so He *could* save us. Jesus knows the Father so well that He was able to teach us just how great God's love is. Jesus gave everything He had, and He even died, so that people could go to heaven and be with Him.

God loved us so much that He gave Jesus to live on earth and then to die for us (John 3:16). People are naturally sinful and do bad things, but God sent Jesus to make us good and pure again. Jesus became a man so that He could show us that He understands what we need. When Jesus became a human being, He became one forever—so we could always know that He is our Brother (Hebrews 2:11). Jesus did all of this so that we would no longer have to be sinful and rebellious—so that we could become loving and holy like God.

A Child of the King

David grabbed Christy's special blanket and started to run. Christy burst out crying. Mrs. Peppers came in to see what was wrong. She called David, sat down in a big chair, and pulled David into her lap.

"David, that was a mean thing to do. You know I don't like it when you do things to upset your sister. No one likes it when you're selfish and hurt other people. You know I still love you, but you must learn to be kind."

David stuck out his lower lip and frowned.

His mother sighed and called Christy to her. "OK, guys, maybe a story will help." By this time, the pages from her folder were tied up in a homemade book. Mrs. Peppers pulled this out to read to her children.

Think about how terrible it was for Jesus to die on the cross. He loves you so much that He was willing to be hurt and killed so that you wouldn't have to hurt and die. Our God's love is so deep and wide that we cannot completely understand it. Because of this big love, you can be sure that God will make you good and happy and holy.

God's love is so good and so big that it will make your heart very happy and full of love for Him. We are God's greatest treasure.

When you believe that Jesus has saved you from your sins, He will make you His own child. He will make you good and holy and righteous. And He will be really proud of you.

Isn't it wonderful? God's love is great. You can be a child of the King. What a lovely promise! Think about it—He loved you before you loved Him. The more you think and learn about God and His love, the more you will understand that His love is like a mother's love for her child, even when her child has done something wrong.

2 I Need Jesus

Trading Hearts

Wednesdays were playground days for David and Christy. Mrs. Peppers usually enjoyed the time talking to the other moms, and she tried to take them every week.

One Wednesday, the children had been playing for a while when they saw Dusty Bradshaw. Dusty’s mother was pushing his baby sister in a stroller. David looked at Dusty and frowned. Christy stood up and left the sand castle she was building to stand on the other side of her mother.

Another girl named Amanda was playing in the sandbox. She didn’t notice as Dusty came running up to the sandpile.

“Can I play?” he shrieked a little louder than he should have.

Amanda squirmed uncomfortably but didn’t leave the sandpile.

Soon the two were playing with cars and sticks and dripping some water from a cup to make streams. Christy stayed by her mother, watching the other kids shyly.

The moms continued to talk to each other. Mrs. Bradshaw started telling some really funny stories. The mothers were laughing when suddenly they heard a shriek of pain.

Ahhhh!

All eyes turned suddenly to Amanda, who was now looking embarrassed. Her mother asked what was wrong, and she said, "Nothing, I'm fine."

A little later David and Christy joined in the fun, helping to create a huge town in the sand. With sticks and leaves, they built houses and a fire station and a church. The children giggled when a carpenter ant walked into their village. They decided to name their new town Antville.

David yelped and came running to his mother. Again, the grown-ups turned quickly to look.

"Mom, Dusty just poked my foot really hard with his stick."

As David was wiping away some tears and a little dribble of blood from his toes, he added, "Dusty always hurts the other kids! He's mean. We tried to like him, but we can't!"

Mrs. Bradshaw guessed what had happened to David—and to Amanda earlier. She gave Dusty an angry look and grabbed him by the hand.

"That's it, young man! We're going home."

She spun him around with one hand and put the baby back in the stroller with the other. As they marched to the car, Dusty screamed in anger. After his mother gave him a serious swat on the bottom, he became quiet. But he was so mad as he walked to the car that he didn't even turn around to say Goodbye.

The moms and the children watched quietly as Mrs. Bradshaw's car pulled out of the gravel parking lot and drove away. Somehow the sandbox didn't seem as much fun anymore. Christy frowned and stuck out her lip. "I don't like him!"

Mrs. Peppers pulled the girl onto her lap and said, "Well, he seems to enjoy bothering people, doesn't he? You know, even though he makes other people unhappy, I think *he's* the one who is the most unhappy. We can do things that are selfish and hurt other people, but it always ends up hurting us more than anyone else."

I Need Jesus

That night Mom pulled out the homemade book and read these words to David and Christy.

In the beginning, people were smart and happy. They were perfect and had pure, loving hearts—just like God's. But because of disobedience, things changed. The minds and hearts of people became wicked and selfish. People became so bad and weak that they didn't even know how to obey. Satan wanted to fill the world with sickness and hurting—and to blame it all on God. Satan trapped people, and they would have been his slaves forever, except that God had a plan.

Before Adam and Eve sinned, they talked face-to-face with God as His special friends. But after they sinned, they were afraid of God. They had disobedient hearts, and God was all good, so they hid from Him.

Even now, most people are afraid of God. They are afraid of His holiness and goodness. Many people think God is boring. Sinners wouldn't be comfortable near God. They would be unhappy when God and His angels were there. Sinners wouldn't be happy in heaven, because people there are kind and caring. Selfish people just can't understand those things.

It would be hard for sinners to feel at home in heaven because they don't like holy things. They would be like sour notes in a pretty song. Sinners would be very unhappy in heaven. They would be so used to doing bad things that they wouldn't have anything to do!

God didn't just make up a rule that wicked people wouldn't be allowed in heaven. They are not allowed there because they wouldn't be happy, and they would make others sad. God's lovely brightness and goodness would be so strange to them that they'd rather die than stay in heaven.

DAVID ASKS WHY

You are a sinner, and so am I. We cannot be freed from the deadly trap of sin by ourselves. We are naturally bad, and there's nothing we can do about it (Job 14:4; Romans 8:7). We can learn about God. We can learn manners and self-control, and these things are nice, but they can't change a bad heart. Those things can even make you seem like a nice person, but they will never give you a good heart.

There *is* Someone, though, who can change a person's heart. Jesus can. When Jesus comes into your heart, you can have a new, good heart. Jesus said that, just like a baby is born as a new life, so every person must let God give them a new heart. Only those with new hearts will ever go to heaven.

Many people think that if they act good, then they can go to heaven. That's not always true. No matter how many good things they do, every person's heart is still rotten and sinful—until God changes it. The Bible

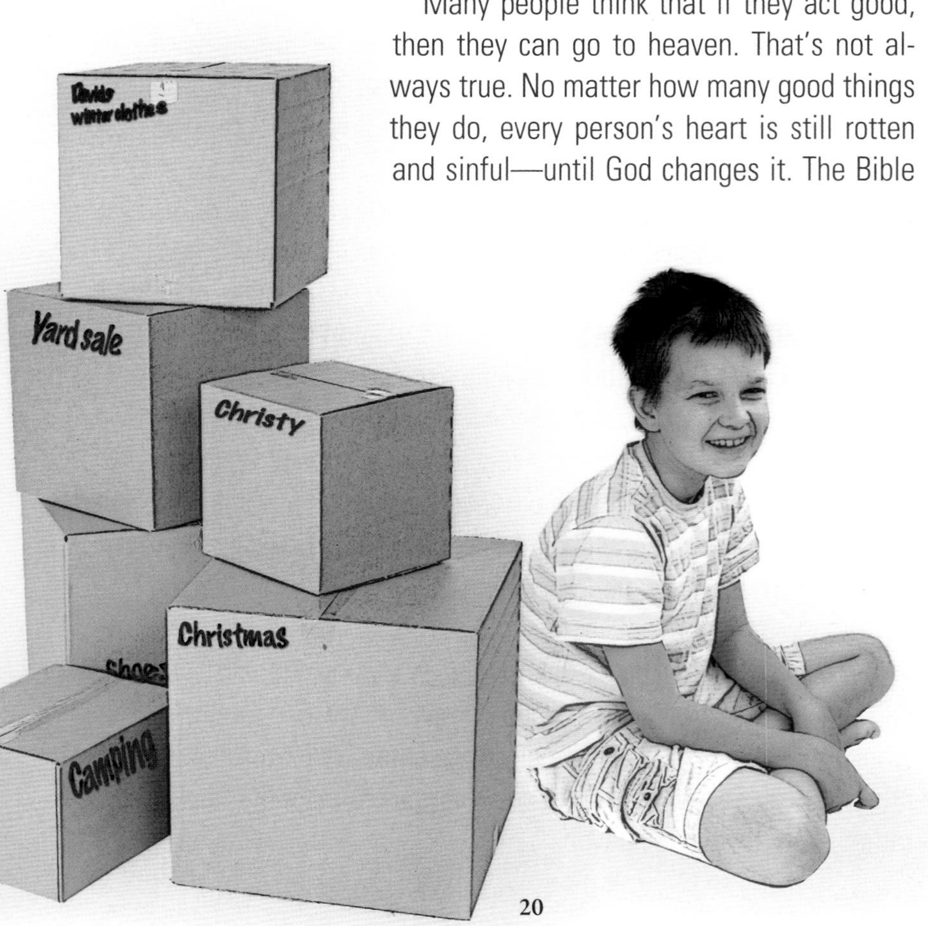

says Jesus is life. When we let Him come into our hearts, He gives us new life. And we will be saved from death.

Do you see how loving and wonderful God is? He is like a kind and wonderful Dad. God is perfect, and His law is fair (Romans 7:16, 12). But just knowing about Him is not good enough. Even though your heart is naturally bad (Romans 7:14), you can ask God to take away your sin and give you a good heart. Do you want to be good and pure and holy? If you look to Jesus, He will take away your sin (John 1:29).

Friends With God

Mrs. Peppers wandered through the house, calling, "David! Christy! Where are you?" She hadn't heard them for a while and was a little worried.

Bang! Boom!

What in the world? She just knew they couldn't be up in the *attic*! Mrs. Peppers went out to the garage to check the attic door, and there she found them. She frowned and put her hands on her hips.

"*What* are you doing?" she asked.

"Oh, hi!" Mr. Peppers called down from the attic. "The kids wanted to help me clean up here. We've got a lot of stuff up here that I haven't seen in a really long time. Should I bring down the baby bed yet?"

"Not yet," Mrs. Peppers said, as she watched David and Christy going up and then down the creaky attic ladder.

"All right, David and Christy, you're making me nervous. Come down."

Both children reluctantly obeyed. They came down to stand beside her on the floor.

DAVID ASKS WHY

"You know," said Mrs. Peppers, "watching you two on that ladder reminds me of a story from the Bible. David, if you run and get our homemade book, I'll read about it to you."

Soon, the three of them were cuddled in their favorite spot, all piled together on the big green chair. This is what they read.

God's Holy Spirit uses many stories and pictures to teach us truth. He wants to make it easy for people to understand who He is.

Many years ago, twin brothers named Jacob and Esau lived in Canaan. Jacob had tricked Esau and taken something very precious. When Esau got angry, Jacob ran away from home. Then he felt terribly guilty!

Poor Jacob was lonely and sad. He missed his family and home very much. But the worst thing was this: he was afraid that God was mad at him and wasn't with him anymore. In sadness, he lay down on the ground and went to sleep.

While Jacob was sleeping, he saw a strange light. He looked across the field and saw a ladder that seemed to lead right up into heaven! God's angels were walking up and down the steps. Jacob heard God speaking from the top. That night God gave Jacob hope and let him know that He still loved him. God told Jacob that Jesus was his Savior from sin and would forgive him. God wanted to be his Friend again! God showed Jacob the ladder to teach him about Jesus. The ladder showed Jacob how God builds a friendship between Himself and people.

When Adam and Eve sinned, they threw away their friendship with God and the angels. Jesus came to this earth to help bring people and God back together again with ties of love. Because Jesus is our Savior, God and the angels can again be our friends. We are weak because of sin, but Jesus connects us with His Father, who is strong. Only with His help can we be strong also.

Many people have plans for how they can become better and stronger and smarter. None of those plans will work until they remember that only Jesus can make us good and strong and smart. Every good thing is a gift straight from God (James 1:17). No one can be really good without Jesus, because He *is* goodness.

God loves you and all His children more than any other thing. When God let Jesus come to earth, They both gave up the very best things They had. Jesus lived and died for you. Now He is praying for you and helping you. The angels help you, and God's Holy Spirit speaks to your heart. Everyone in heaven loves you. Their job is to help save you from sin. They want to be with you in heaven.

Think about all God has done for us! Thank Jesus for all the loving work He is doing to save you. You will have the happiness of heaven and the angels for your friends. You can have a close friendship with Jesus and with God, your heavenly Father. You'll have a chance to grow and learn forever. Those are wonderful reasons to work for God. Won't you give your heart to Jesus and choose to obey Him?

Now if we obey Satan, the only things we will get in the end are God's sadness and punishment. Sin makes an ugly, wicked heart. Someday, those who obey Satan will die forever.

Let's pay attention to God's kindness. He gave us all that He could. He has loved us *so* much. Let's invite Jesus into our hearts, and He will make us holy and good like He is. When we do, we can be sure that the angels will be our friends. God, our Father, and Jesus, His Son, will be our very dearest Friends in the world.

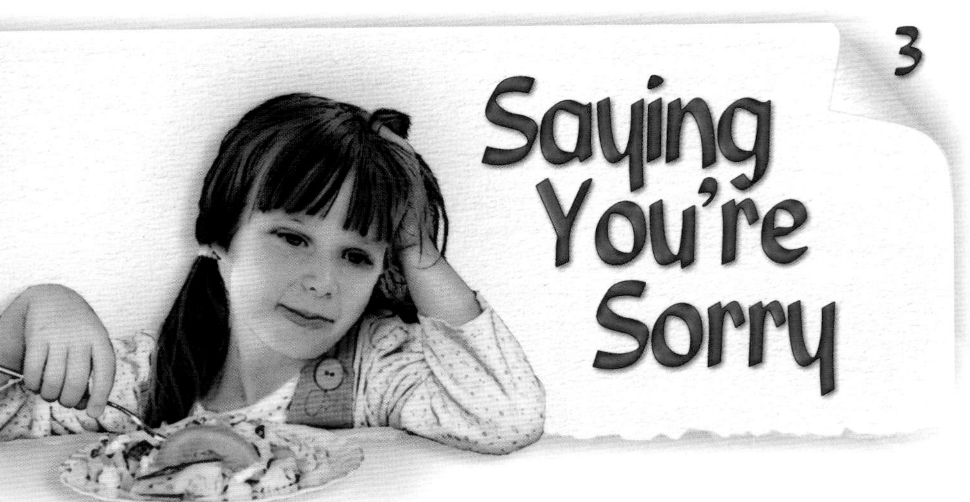

Why Are You Sorry?

The family was sitting around the table sharing stories when Mr. Peppers noticed that Christy was pushing her salad around on her plate. "Christy, please stop playing with your food. You'll make a mess."

Christy looked up with just her eyes and stuffed a little bite into her mouth.

The conversation continued, but Christy wasn't a part of it. She was busy playing with a spoon on the edge of her plate, trying to see if she could scoop up the lettuce.

Dad frowned and took her spoon away. "OK, use your fork. You've got to stop playing with your food."

With a sheepish grin, Christy whispered, "OK, Dad." But after taking another bite or two, she forgot again and started to turn her plate around and around.

Crash!

Mom jumped. David jumped. Dad jumped and picked up Christy while Mom tried to gather up the lettuce and tomatoes and broken glass.

Christy stared at the scattered mess with wide eyes for a

moment; then she started to cry. "I'm s-s-s-sorry!"

After the mess was cleaned up and the others were eating again, Christy pulled her glass of juice to the edge of the table and tried to lift it up with her teeth.

"Christy!" Dad said sharply. "What are you doing? You said you were sorry. If you were really sorry, you would stop what you're doing."

Since everyone was almost finished eating, Mrs. Peppers interrupted, "All right, everyone, let's go to the other room. It's story time."

How can you be holy? How can you be good when you have a bad heart? Only Jesus can make us truly good. He can make us friends with God. But how will He do that? The Bible teaches us how to come to Jesus. The first thing it says to do is to repent (Acts 2:37, 38). When you tell Jesus that you're sorry for being bad, He will forgive your sin (Acts 3:19).

To repent means two things. The first is to feel sorry for the bad things you've done. And the second is to choose to obey God and stop doing those things. Unless you decide to do both, your heart will never change.

Many people don't understand what it means to repent. They are kind of sorry for being bad, and then they try to be good because they are afraid of being punished. That is not what the Bible is talking about when it tells us to repent. These people are sad and sorry about the getting punished instead of sorry about the bad things that they have done.

Sometimes people say they are sorry because they are afraid or because they hope to get something good out of it. But their hearts haven't changed at all. That is not what the Bible means by repentance either.

DAVID ASKS WHY

Judas was the wicked man who betrayed Jesus. He knew he had sinned, but he admitted that only because he was afraid of getting into trouble. He knew he would have to be punished for his wicked deed, so he was scared. He was never truly sorry for helping to kill Jesus. Almost anyone will *say* they are sorry so they don't have to be punished, but we should actually *be* sorry for the bad things we've done. We should be sad that we hurt Jesus.

God's Holy Spirit is working on our hearts, and when we let Him help us, He will show us the difference between good and bad. He will show us how good God is and how bad sin is. We will understand God's greatness and love. He will show us God's love and beautiful holiness. We will want to be pure and to be God's friend!

King David did something really bad, and he was sorry. He prayed, asking God to forgive him. His prayer shows us what it means to be really sorry for sin. David was really sorry and didn't make any excuses for what he had done. He saw that he had a bad heart. He hated the bad things he'd done and wanted to be forgiven, but he also wanted a new, clean heart. He wanted the happy feeling that comes from being good. He wanted to be a close friend with God again. Here is the prayer he prayed to God:

> Have mercy on me, dear God!
> I know You are loving and kind.
> I know You love to be nice.
> Scratch out all my sins—I know I've been bad!
> I think about my sin all the time.
> Wash my ugly heart, and I will be clean and pure.
> Give me a new heart, O God. Make it strong and patient.
> Let me stay near You; give me Your Holy Spirit.
> I used to be happy because You saved me—please
> make me happy again.

Saying You're Sorry

Hold me up and forgive me for hurting people.
Oh God, You have saved me, and I will sing songs about
Your goodness

(Psalm 51:1–14).

Another time, King David said, "You can be happy when God forgives your sins and takes them away. You can be happy when God doesn't see your sin anymore, and when you have an honest heart" (Psalm 32:1, 2).

King David truly repented, but no one can really repent and be sorry by himself. Jesus can help us and show us how to really be sorry; He will change our hearts.

Everything Good Is From Jesus

David and Pablo were squatting on the sidewalk, playing a new game with sidewalk chalk and smooth rocks when Gordo came up to join the fun.

The two smaller boys jumped up and turned away. As they started to go into the house, David whispered, "That Gordo is a bad boy!"

Mrs. Peppers overheard David. She asked in surprise, "What do you mean?"

The boys frowned, and David said, "Gordo's awful! He tells really scary stories and is mean almost all the time. We don't want to play with him."

Mom's face grew softer. "Oh, David! I know that people are sometimes hard to get along with. You don't have to be Gordo's best friend, but, you know what? All of us have bad hearts. We have no business being rude or talking bad about people. How do you expect Gordo ever to be nice if you don't show him Jesus? None of us are good in ourselves, but Jesus can help us be good. And He can help Gordo, too, but He needs us to love Gordo for Him!"

DAVID ASKS WHY

Many people think that when they have done something bad, they have to be sorry before they can come to Jesus. That is not true! It *is* true that repentance makes us ready to receive forgiveness because unless we are sad about our sins, we won't even know we need Jesus. But do we have to be sorry before we can come to Jesus?

No. The Bible says that we can come to Jesus right now. We don't have to wait until we feel sorry. Jesus' goodness will help us be truly sorry. He will help us feel sorry, and then He will forgive us and heal us. We can never repent without Jesus to help us.

Whenever someone wants to do something good, it is because Jesus put that feeling in his or her heart. Jesus is the reason sin is hateful to us. Do you want to be true and clean? Do you see that your own heart is bad? That's because the Spirit of Jesus is speaking to your heart.

Saying You're Sorry

Jesus said that if we get people to think about Him, He will attract people to Himself (John 12:32). We must teach people that Jesus is the One who can save them and that He died for everyone's sins. As we think about Jesus dying on the cross like an innocent little lamb, we will begin to know the secret of how He saves us, and God's goodness will lead us to really feel sorry for our sin.

Sometimes people are ashamed of their bad ways, and they stop some of their bad habits even before they realize that Jesus is leading them. But if they really want to do right and are trying to be better, it's because Jesus is making them feel that way. The Holy Spirit is softly working on their heart, and they don't even know it. Their hearts wake up deep down inside, and they begin to change. They see how sinful they are. They begin to see how good Jesus is and how horrible sin is. They begin to understand God's love.

We can fight against this love if we want to, but if we don't, Jesus will bring us close to His heart. When we understand how He saves us, we will go to Jesus with a sad feeling for our sins, because we will understand that our sins hurt Him.

God is talking to people's hearts and making them hungry for something they don't have. Nothing in the whole world will fill them up with what they need. God's Holy Spirit is begging them to look for the only thing that can make them happy and give them security.

Sin can be fun for a while, but it leaves us sad and empty. Jesus is trying to lead our hearts away from those things and to give us all the joys we can have in Him. Jesus has a special message to everyone who is hoping for something better. He says, "Are you thirsty? Come and drink the water of life—drink as much as you want" (Revelation 22:17).

Does your heart need something that nothing in the world can give you? Do you feel empty? If so, this is God's voice calling to your heart. Ask Him to help you be sorry for your sins. Ask Him to show you the love and sweetness of Jesus.

Jesus showed us how to keep God's law perfectly. He loved to share and was never selfish. When we look at Jesus, we'll see that our own hearts are selfish.

Do you think you're pretty good? Do you think that your life is OK? Do you look at bad people and thank God you're not that bad? When light from Jesus shines into your heart, you will see the truth—that you actually have an unclean heart. He will help you see that you are naturally selfish and are an enemy of God. Nothing we do is really good. Everything good that we try to do is like a dirty rag (Isaiah 64:6). But Jesus can clean us up. He can give us new hearts just like His!

When God shines His holiness into our hearts, we will see just how unclean we are. We will see that our hearts are not good or healthy. We will see that the things we want aren't always good and that our hearts don't belong completely to God. God will show us where we break His law, and this will make us sad. When we understand what we're really like, we won't like ourselves very much. Jesus is so pure and bright that we'll see only our sins.

When we see how awesome God is, we will hate our own selfishness. Instead, we will want to have the pure, lovely hearts that Jesus promises to give us. He will teach us to be His friend and to keep His holy law.

Who Makes You Good?

It was a warm afternoon for Christmastime. David's family and a couple of other families had bundled into jackets and were going around the church neighborhood, giving books about Jesus to the people they met.

Laurie was just about David's age. She and David were walking together with Laurie's mom, while Dad and Christy were on the other side of the street.

"Don't walk on the grass, Laurie," her mom said. "It's muddy. Come out of the grass."

Laurie made an ugly face and stepped onto a little dry bush in the flower bed.

Crunch!

"Laurie! That's not what I meant! Get out of the flower bed."

Laurie grumpily stepped onto the sidewalk and whispered something mean to David.

David's eyes got big because of what she said, but he swallowed hard and didn't say anything. He glanced at her mom to see if she had heard, but she was busy giving a book to an old lady who had come to the door. It didn't look as if Laurie's mom had noticed what Laurie had said.

A little while later, Laurie started complaining that her feet hurt. David didn't say anything about her silly, grown-up looking shoes, but he thought his feet would be hurting, too, if he had to wear them.

As he and Laurie were getting ready to cross the street to the next group of houses, they saw someone coming down the side road.

"Yuk!" Laurie gasped. "See that guy coming this way? I'll bet he stinks!"

As the bearded old man came closer, he smiled at Laurie. But she made a face and ran past him to her dad, who was nearby.

David hardly noticed Laurie. He ran up to the old man and gave him a hug.

"Hi, Mr. Greg! Mom said if we saw you today, I could invite you to eat lunch with us tomorrow. Can you come?" He handed Mr. Greg one of his little books. "She told me not to tell you that we made you a *really cool* present."

The man's wrinkled face broke into a yellow-toothed grin.

"Sure, if your mom's cooking, I'll be there!"

Later, on the way home, David told Mom and Dad what had happened with Laurie and Mr. Greg. "You know, Laurie and I go to the same class at church, and she can answer all the questions about Jesus, but I'd rather be Mr. Greg's friend. Sometimes I think Laurie stinks more than he does—even if she does wear her birthday perfume!"

Mrs. Peppers smiled. "You know, some people have really big problems. They may look bad or not seem very lovable. At the same time, other people may look and smell just fine, but are downright mean!" She pulled out the book to read.

Paul was a very important preacher in the Bible. He knew all about God's law and was very proud of himself because he thought he kept it perfectly (Philippians 3:6). But when he began to understand that the law was all about God and not all about him, he was sad and ashamed. When he saw that the law was supposed to be in his heart—not just rules telling him what he was supposed to do—he realized that he was really a sinner, and he couldn't be proud of himself anymore.

Saying You're Sorry

Some sins displease God more than other sins. But even if something seems like only a small sin to people, God doesn't see it that way. He sees sins as they really are.

Have you ever seen a drunk person? People often think that a drunk man is terribly wicked. They say that he will never go to heaven. But God thinks some sins are much, much worse than being drunk. Some people think they're better than everyone else. Some people are very selfish, always wanting the biggest and best of everything. God sees these sins as very bad because He is unselfish and loving.

If a person gets drunk or does something else that we think is terribly bad, he will probably feel very sorry and ashamed afterward. But a person who thinks he or she is better than everyone else or is selfish might not even realize that selfishness is a sin! So selfishness and pride are very dangerous sins because most of the time selfish, proud people don't feel they need to come to Jesus. They don't think they really need Jesus, even though He came to give them more good things than they can imagine.

Jesus told a story about a tax collector and a teacher who went to church one Sabbath and prayed (Luke 18:13). Nobody liked the tax collector, so he stood in a corner and prayed quietly to God. He knew he was a wicked man, so he begged for God to have pity on him. His heart was open for God to set him free and to heal him from sin.

The teacher was very proud of himself. He thanked God, because he thought he was very holy, when actually, he was very selfish. He thought he was so great that he wasn't even listening when God spoke to His heart. He was far from God and didn't really know what God was like, so he couldn't see how bad he was. He didn't ask God for help and holiness when he prayed—so he didn't get anything from God.

Do you see that you are a sinner? Don't wait and try to make yourself better. A lot of people think they are too bad to come to Jesus. Do you think you can make yourself good if you try really hard? "Can a person change the color of his skin? Can a leopard erase his spots? Of course not! And you are so used to doing bad things, that you can't be good either" (Jeremiah 13:23). Only God can help you. Don't wait to change until your heart is burning or until you feel like being good. Come to Jesus now, just like you are.

Don't be fooled, though. Some people think that God is so loving and kind that He will save everyone, even those who refuse to be His friends. God knows how bad sin really is. Sin is so bad that it killed Jesus on a cross. Do you think that God is so nice that He will never punish bad people? Sin was so bad that God had to let His own Son die! We can never clean up our hearts by ourselves. We can never get to heaven by ourselves. That's why Jesus took our sins and died instead of us.

If we think about all the love it took for Jesus to die for us, we'll understand just how terrible sin really is. Then we will know that the only way to be free from sin and to get to heaven is to give our hearts to Jesus and be willing to obey Him.

If people aren't really sorry for their sins, they look at Christians and say, "I'm just as good as they are. They aren't any better than I am; they aren't more holy. They're just as selfish as I am!" They think that just because other people are sometimes bad, it's OK for them to be bad too. But Jesus never asked us to look at other Christians and be like them. He wants us to be like Him! If you believe that Christians should be good, go to Jesus so that *you* can be good!

Little Sins

David was supposed to be taking a nap, but he had chewed a hole in his sheet. When Mom came into his room and saw what he had done, she was upset. "Why do you keep doing that?" she asked.

David thought it was funny; he wanted to show her the pattern the hole had made—kind of a decoration. Somehow Mom didn't think it was very funny. "You know, David," Mom said, "I have asked you not to do this, and that should be enough."

"Why are you mad? It's just a little hole!"

"David, don't you know that if you disobey just a little bit, then it becomes easier to disobey the next time? If you choose to disobey just a little bit, disobedience will grow."

She sat down on the side of his bed and sighed. "David, Jesus wants you to be free and happy. Please don't be stubborn. Let's read tonight's story right now."

Jesus wants you to give up your sins and ask for a clean heart—don't wait until it's too late! Lots of people have waited and waited, thinking they would give their hearts to Jesus soon. But the time never came, and they waited until it was too late. If you decide to wait to come to Jesus, you're really choosing to keep being bad, and this is dangerous. It doesn't matter how small your sin is, you must let Jesus have it. If you don't let the sin go, it will end up hurting you and finally killing you.

Adam and Eve just ate a little piece of fruit in the Garden. God told them not to eat any of it, but they thought it was such a little thing that it didn't matter. But that little thing broke God's holy law and pulled them away from God. That one little sin opened up the door for sickness and death.

That happened a long time ago, but ever since then, there has been crying and sadness all over earth. Even the angels in heaven are sad because of how wicked people are. They lost a lot when their dear Jesus came to earth and died on the cross. Don't ever think that sin is just a little thing.

Every time you sin—every single time you decide to ignore what Jesus wants from you—it hurts you. It makes your heart hard and makes it harder for you to understand the Bible. When you say No to Jesus, it makes it easier to say No to Him the next time.

Do you think you can change whenever you want to? Do you think Jesus will always make you feel bad when you do something wrong? If you keep on doing the bad things you like to do, it won't be so easy to change later. The things you do work on your heart. The more you are bad, the more you want to be bad. And someday, when Jesus calls to your heart, you may not even care!

Jesus wants us to give Him everything bad. If we try to hold on to even one little sin, someday it will push Jesus all the way out of our hearts. Every time we sin, it gets harder to obey. Don't play with sin; don't keep it around. If you don't give it to Jesus now, someday it will trap you (Proverbs 5:22).

Jesus wants to make us free, but He won't make us give Him our sins. If we keep being stubborn and don't want to be free, there's nothing He can do! If we keep saying No to His love, we will only hurt ourselves. Now is the right time (2 Corinthians 6:2), the very best time, to choose to listen to Jesus and give Him our hearts (Proverbs 5:22).

The way we look, the things we say and do, the kind of clothes we wear—all these things are important to people. But do you know what's important to God? Your heart. Sometimes we're happy, and sometimes we're sad. Our hearts change all the time. God knows what our hearts are all about. He knows everything we want to do and why we feel the way we do.

Saying You're Sorry

Go to God with your unclean heart. Open up your secrets and let God take a look at you. Do you want God to know you well? Do you want Him to understand when you're afraid? If you ask for His help, He will always show you just what to do.

A lot of people think it's enough to *act* like a Christian—even if the heart is not changed. But you should pray, "Dear God, give me a brand-new, clean heart! Make my spirit right with You again" (Psalm 51:10).

Be honest with yourself. Make sure you really know that you love God and that you will do whatever He asks. If you just *look* like a Christian but you never let Jesus give you a good heart, then someday you will die.

Listen to Bible stories and really think about what Jesus is saying to you. The Bible tells us about God's law and the life of Jesus. It will teach you how to really be good and how to go to heaven (Hebrews 12:14). The Bible teaches you what things are bad, but it also shows you how to be saved! Listen to God—He's calling you!

Don't Give Up!

"She drives me crazy! She's always messing up my stuff," David yelled.

Mrs. Peppers came in to find out what was wrong. David was angrily putting all his things up where Christy couldn't reach them.

"David! Calm down!"

"Mom," said David, "I don't want to be bad, but sometimes I lose my temper with Christy. Sometimes I think I'm just bad and don't really want to be a Christian!"

"Run get our book, David. I think today's story will be just in time."

DAVID ASKS WHY

Do you know that you've been bad? Don't give up! If you are a sinner, then you are just the one that Jesus wants to save! We don't have to try to make God our Friend; Jesus died just so we could be right with God again (2 Corinthians 5:19). He's calling lovingly to our hearts. He's more loving and kind than even a wonderful mom or dad, and when we make mistakes, He is very patient. He promises to help us and offers for us to be His friends, because He loves us more than anyone else does.

Satan likes to make we think that we are very bad. When he tempts us like this, we can talk about how good Jesus is. When we think about Jesus and His love, it will help us. Tell Satan, "I know I have sinned. But Jesus came to save people just like me, and I know that He will help me because He loves me!" (1 Timothy 1:15).

Simon was a very important man who was a friend of Jesus. One day, Jesus told him a story. "Once upon a time," Jesus said, "there were three men. One of these men was very rich ruler, and the other two were his servants. One of the servants borrowed a little bit of money from the ruler, and the other servant borrowed a lot of money. Later, they both felt very bad because neither could pay him back. So, the ruler decided to be nice. He said that neither one of the men had to give him back the money. They were both happy."

Then Jesus asked Simon, "Which servant do you think was the happiest?" Simon knew right away. "The one that owed his master the most money" (Luke 7:43).

We are like those two men, and God is like the ruler. Because we have sinned, we owe Him everything. But Jesus died, so that everything would be taken care of and our debt would be paid.

Saying You're Sorry

Have you been bad? Then you can be very happy that God has forgiven you. When you get to heaven, you can stand very close to God and sing happy songs to Him. When you understand just how much He has given to save you, you will be happier and happier forever.

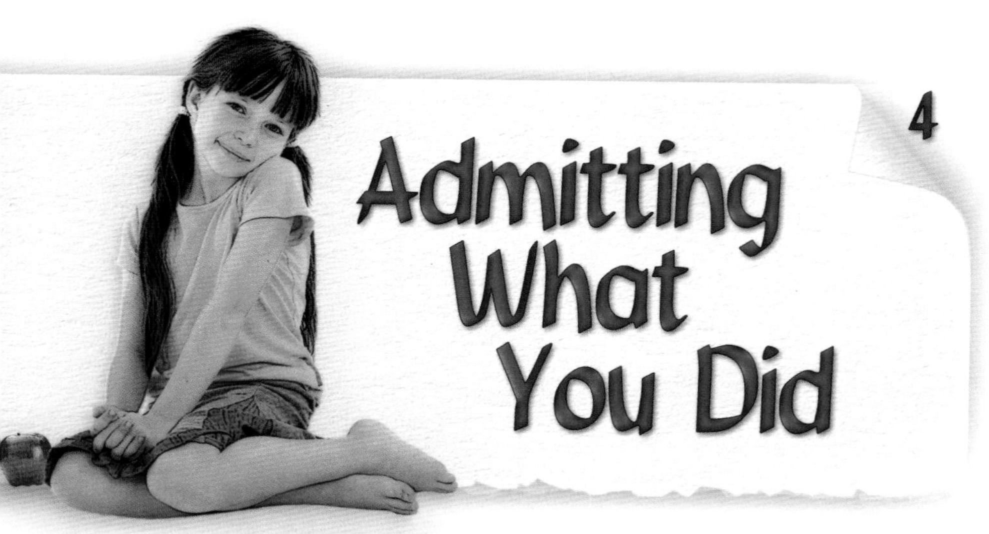

4 Admitting What You Did

The First Step

Mrs. Peppers was feeling sick again. David was trying to keep Christy busy in the other room. They'd been having fun. But when David got back from the bathroom, he saw Christy hide something behind her back.

"What's that, Christy?"

"Nothing!" she said loudly.

Mrs. Peppers got up and came into the room. Right away she noticed sticky juice running down Christy's chin and chunks of white around her mouth.

"Christy," her mother said. "What have you been into?"

"Nothing!" Christy said. But her chin and lips were shaking. She kept her hands behind her back and started to walk backward toward the door.

David came closer. "Christy, if you just tell Mom, she won't be so mad. Don't lie!"

Christy looked down. "Apple," she whispered. Her hands came from behind her back. She gave the half-eaten fruit to her mother.

Mrs. Peppers picked up a package of wipes and cleaned Christy's messy face.

"All right, Christy, thank you for telling the truth. You know that you're not to get into the refrigerator without permission! I'm glad you admitted what you did, though. You know the thoughts in your mind that told you to do the right thing? That's Jesus speaking to you. You should always listen and obey when Jesus tells you what to do!

"Well, it's about time for lunch," Mrs. Peppers continued. "But let's read first. Today's story just might help you feel better."

"Don't try to hide your sin—you'll never win that way! Tell Jesus all about your sin, and then give it up! He will be kind" (Proverbs 28:13).

Do you want God to forgive you? There are a few things you have to do, but they are easy and fair. And they really make sense. God doesn't want us to do some hard thing to make up for all the bad things we've done. Some people think God will love them more if they take long trips to special places or if they hurt or punish themselves.

James was one of Jesus' special friends. He teaches us that if we do something bad, we must say that we're sorry and pray for each other (James 5:16). When we tell God all about it and tell our friends we're sorry for what we did, God will forgive us!

Do you know that God made everyone? Everybody is a special treasure in God's eyes, so when we hurt someone, we must tell that person we're sorry, but we need to be sure to tell God that we're sorry too. If we hurt our friend or our brother or sister, it makes Jesus hurt too. Jesus knows every time we do something bad, but He is very kind. He understands what it's like to be tempted, and He can clean up our dirty, bad hearts.

So the very first step to getting right with God is to admit that we've been bad. We must see how bad it is to sin, and we must feel sad for hurting Jesus. Just because we think Jesus is our Friend doesn't mean we will have a happy heart. We must ask for one. We must ask God to give us His quiet happiness.

There is only one reason God cannot forgive people. He cannot forgive them if they won't admit they've done something bad! If we've done something to hurt God, we must go to Him and say we're sorry. If we've done something to hurt our friends or family, we need to ask for their forgiveness. But it does no good if we don't really mean it. When we understand how very bad sin is, we know how sad it makes our Father in heaven. God can make us feel sad about what we've done if we ask Him, and then afterward, He will make us happier than ever.

If we choose to stop our bad ways and ask Jesus to help us be winners, we can be sure He will be very close to our hearts. He saves people who are sorry for their sins (Psalm 34:18).

Making Things Right

Mr. and Mrs. Peppers and their children went to the river with their new friend Emily and her dad. David and his father had walked down the path. They were looking at a strange water bug. Mrs. Peppers and Christy were sitting on the riverbank near Emily.

Christy was amazed as she watched Emily's dad cast his fishing line into the water at just the right spot. But she was even more amazed when he pulled out a cigarette and started smoking.

"That's bad!" Christy gasped. "Don't you know that will make you sick?"

"No way!" Emily's dad said, laughing. "Smoking doesn't make you sick! It actually calms you down and helps you not get grumpy."

Christy stayed quiet after that. But she remembered that Emily's father *had* been grumpy on the way to the river. Her own dad was almost never grumpy or mean.

Later, at home, Christy asked her father if what Emily's dad had said was true. "Does smoking really help you be calm and happy?"

"Well, Christy," Dad began, "I've known Emily's dad for many years—since a long time before you were born. He actually used to know that smoking can make you sick. But he wanted to keep doing it. So he stopped thinking about how bad cigarettes are for your health. Eventually he forgot what he knew. Before long, he was smoking all the time. Now he doesn't even realize that smoking *will* make him sick someday.

"Let's go get our homemade book," Mr. Peppers said to Christy. "I think Mom's story for today talks about this."

If you really are sorry for something you've done, you'll talk to the one you've hurt and tell that person just what you're sorry about.

A prophet is a person God talks to in a special way. The prophet tells people about the messages God has for them. A long time ago, God's special people, the Israelites, had a prophet named Samuel.

The Israelites were having many hard times, and Samuel told them it was because they didn't trust in God anymore. They wanted a king because they didn't think God was doing a good enough job taking care of them. Well, this made God very sad because *He* wanted to be their only King! The Israelites continued to be very sad until they finally realized their own silliness and wickedness and said, "We did many bad things before, but now we've been really bad, because we asked for a King instead of God" (1 Samuel 12:19).

God had been a good King, but the people were not thankful. Their hearts were sad, and they couldn't be friends with God again until they told Him just what they were sorry for.

It's never good enough to just say, "I'm sorry," and then go on doing the same things you did before. Your life just has to change. If you know something hurts dear Jesus, you must be willing to give it up. If you really are sorry, you will not want to be bad anymore—and Jesus can make you a winner!

God is good at washing sins away from our dirty hearts. He will give our hearts a bath if we are willing. He tells us to stop doing the bad things that we've been doing, and He promises to make us good and clean again. He wants us to be honest and helpful and kind (Isaiah 1:16, 17). If we give back anything we've taken and do what God asks us to do, we will live forever! (Ezekiel 33:15).

Sometimes people do bad things for so long that they don't even know those things are bad anymore! The Spirit of God is working on their hearts, trying to get them to listen. They must obey, or they'll never understand how much God hates sin. Sometimes people make excuses. They say, "Well, I never would have done that if this person hadn't made me mad." If someone corrects them for what they've done, they want to blame it on someone else.

When the very first man and woman, Adam and Eve, ate the fruit that God told them not to touch, they felt embarrassed and afraid. They knew that they must die, but they didn't want to. When God tried to talk to Adam about his disobedience, Adam blamed it on Eve. Then Eve said that the snake had tricked her and it was all his fault. Then she blamed God for making the snake!

Satan loves for us to blame our bad choices on other people. It's not good enough to say we are sorry—and then blame it partly on someone else. If we're *really* sorry, we'll take the blame and the punishment. We won't make excuses. We won't be proud, but will share our sad heart with Jesus. He will forgive us because we belong to Him.

We must think about Jesus. Think about how He died for us on a cross. Then our hearts will be sad about what we have done. And if we are truly sad about what we have done, Jesus will forgive us and save us.

5 Sticking With It

Looking for God

Mrs. Peppers had been sick a lot during the past few months, and David just didn't understand. His mother and father had told him that a new baby was coming, but he didn't understand why that had to make his mom feel bad all the time.

"David," Mrs. Peppers explained, "you remember how I was sick and had to have surgery when you were little. I'm not really strong enough to have a baby growing inside me, so now I'm sick and often don't feel very well. But aren't you still happy about the baby?"

"I guess so. I just think I'd be awfully grumpy if I were you! But I have a question."

Mrs. Peppers raised her eyebrows, not sure what to think about his serious face. "Yes?"

"Since God made the baby, did He make you sick? Aren't you mad at God?"

She smiled. "No, God didn't make me sick. And I'm not mad at Him. In a way, I'm glad, because feeling bad is teaching me that I can still be happy and learn to obey Jesus even when

I don't always feel like it. Now I know that God is bigger and stronger than I ever understood before. Does that make sense?"

While David was thinking about what his mom had said, Mrs. Peppers called Christy, and the three of them sat down together to read.

God promises that when we search for Him with our whole heart, we *will* find Him (Jeremiah 29:13).

When God first made Adam and Eve, they were very much like Him. Do you want to be like God? Then you must give your heart to Him.

Of course, it's often easier to be bad than to be good. That's because sin has made us have sick hearts. Sin has made us not strong enough to be good. Satan has trapped us. But God wants to set us free. If we choose to obey, God will make us free and strong. He will change our entire hearts and lives.

There have been lots of wars and fights in the world. But the toughest fight ever is the fight to give ourselves to Jesus. Satan tries to tell us that it's fun to sin. We must choose to give our hearts back to Jesus even when it seems hard to do that.

Satan wants us to believe that God is just mean and bossy. But that's not true! God gives us His ways that will help us be happy, and we must choose whether or not to obey. He will never *make* us obey because then we'd never grow and learn to truly love Him.

God doesn't want us to be robots; He wants us to be His friends. That's why He made us! If we choose to obey Him, we will learn to understand the many gifts He has tucked away just for us. We will have the happy freedom that every friend of God receives.

Sticking With It

It's up to you. You may choose to be stuck in Satan's trap or to be happy and free as God's special child. You can be stuck in selfishness and laziness, or you can give yourself completely to God. By giving yourself to God, you become His own child.

Some people say that they are friends of God, while they are trying very hard to obey His rules on their own. They think that if they try hard enough, they'll be good enough to go heaven. They try to act like Christians, but unless their heart is completely changed by how much they love Jesus, they are not really Christians at all!

When Jesus lives in our hearts, we will be full of His love. We will love to pray to Him and spend time with Him. When we learn to think about Jesus, we won't think about ourselves so much. When that happens, Jesus can teach us to do all sorts of wonderful things.

Some people do only what they think they have to do to make God happy. God's love makes us want to do as much as we can for Him and for other people. If people say that they are Christians, but are not kind and loving and giving, they are actually not Christians at all—just very unhappy people.

Do you feel like it's too hard to give your heart to Jesus? Does it seem too hard to obey? Well, remember this: Jesus lived on this earth for you and let people hurt Him so that you could escape this sinful world! We don't deserve God's love, but He loves us anyway. Don't you want to give to your heart to Him? He's given us so many good presents that sometimes it's easy to forget how bad we really are. Think about Jesus and the hard life He lived for you. Then don't complain when your life seems hard.

Do you think you are a pretty good person? Jesus still wants you to be sorry when you are bad. He never did anything bad, and yet He was sorry about sin. He let everyone think He was bad. He took our punishment so that He could save you!

It doesn't have to be so hard to give our hearts to Jesus. Our hearts are dirty, and He wants to clean them. So don't be afraid to give Him your heart. Choose to be happy, and He will help you.

Choices, Choices

"Don't walk there! Stay on the path, please."

A few minutes later, Mrs. Peppers had to say it again. "Stay on the sand, please, David. Christy! Don't go near there; you'll touch poison ivy."

David and Christy looked at each other and then at their mother with wide eyes. They chose to obey even though it was winter and there were no leaves anywhere. They wanted to go off the path, but they paid attention to what their mom had told them. They stayed on the path the rest of the way.

Mrs. Peppers could tell that they were really trying to obey, and she laughed out loud because it made her think of something. "That reminds me of a story," she said to David and Christy. "When I was younger—before you were born, and before I even met your dad, I was

a counselor and teacher at a summer camp. I had so much fun that year!

"Well, one week, my little cousin, Timothy, came to camp. I was teaching a class about which plants and flowers in the woods are safe to eat. Timothy decided that would be a fun class to take.

"One day when he was walking to supper with the other kids in his cabin, Timothy thought he would show all his friends that he was really tough and cool. He grabbed a handful of leaves growing on a vine by the road and shouted, 'Look! This is poison ivy, but it won't hurt me!' He stuffed the leaves into his mouth, and while he friends stood watching, he swallowed them!

"His counselor was very angry and very scared. He rushed Timothy to the nurse, who was even more scared. She knew that such a dumb trick could be very dangerous. But before they took Timothy to the hospital, they decided to call me.

"I asked the counselor to take me to the plant that Timothy had eaten. I saw that it wasn't poison ivy after all and that the plant he had eaten would just give him a bellyache. So, he didn't get a trip to the hospital, but he did get in huge trouble."

David and Christy could hardly stop giggling the rest of the walk. But they stayed on the path.

When they arrived home, Mrs. Peppers pulled out the homemade book to read.

Sometimes God asks us to give up something we like. But remember that He never asks us to give up something that He knows is really good for us. He just wants to give us what is best.

Sticking With It

God has the very best ideas for us. Wouldn't it be great if everyone understood the fun and happiness that God has in mind for them if they choose to obey Him? When we decide to disobey God, we always end up getting hurt. If God made a rule and we said No to Him, we would never be really happy until we decided to obey. God made us, and He knows what will make us happy. When we disobey, we will always end up hurt and miserable.

Do you sometimes think that God likes it when you're sad or hurting? That's *not true*! God and all the angels want us to be happy. God loves to teach us all how to be happy. All God's rules are His ways to teach us how to be happy. They are His ways that keep us away from things that will make us sad.

Do you know what? God knows just how naughty we are. He understands that our hearts are not clean. But if we choose to give our hearts to Him and if we choose to obey, He will clean our hearts right up with love and happiness. He will give peace to our bothered hearts. He knows that when we obey, we will be happier than we've ever been efore. When Jesus is truly in our hearts, *then* we will be completely happy.

Do you wonder *how* to give your unclean mind to God? Do you want to know *how* to give your heart to Jesus? Maybe you want to be good, but being bad seems more fun. Maybe you're so used to doing naughty things that you don't even remember to do good anymore.

Have you promised to be good before? It didn't work very well for long, did it? You don't know *how* to think better thoughts or do better things. You may think that you'll never be really good, or maybe that God doesn't even like you. Don't feel sad!

We need to understand a very important word, and that word is *choice.* When we decide to obey or to disobey, that is making a choice. God has made us able to *choose,* but the choices we make are ours. We can't obey God or even love Him without special help. But we can *choose* to obey Him, and when we do, *then* He will make us strong to obey. This is how Jesus becomes our King. Once we choose to give our hearts to Jesus, He will give us His own good heart.

It's nice to *want* to be good and holy, but if that's where it stops, it's really not enough. Not everyone who just wants to be a Christian will go to heaven. If we want to go to heaven, we must decide to let God make the choices.

If we let Jesus make the choices, our whole lives will be changed. When we let Jesus make our choices, He will be our strong Helper. He is stronger than anyone else. When we choose to give our choices to Jesus, He will teach us how to be real, trusting Christians.

6 Believe and Receive

A New Heart, a New Start

David and Christy wiggled in Dad's lap, trying to get a better look at the ultrasound. They were so excited to watch the baby moving. The technician showed them the tiny fingers and toes on the big black-and-white monitor. They got to see the funny-looking face and then the heart. The technician moved the big white stick over Mom's tummy and pointed to the screen at the four parts of the heart.

"See how the heart is flashing? That's a good thing! It means the baby's heart is working just right."

Later, at home, they were looking at the pictures the technician had printed for them and trying to find all the parts. One picture showed the parts of the heart.

"You know," Mom said, "this pretty little boy has a brand-new heart. I'll bet a lot of people would like to have a new heart again. A lot of people would love to have a new mind, a new way of thinking. Do you know that God promises a new heart for us if we want it?"

David knew what was coming, so he ran to the bookshelf and grabbed the book.

Have you ever heard of a *conscience*? When you in feel in your heart that you should be good or that you shouldn't do something wrong—that's God's Spirit talking to you. That is called your *conscience.*

When our hearts, or *consciences,* begin to help us see how bad sin is, we will learn to hate sin as a terrible thing. Our *consciences* help us see that sin has taken us far away from God and has trapped us. If we try to stop being bad, we'll find out

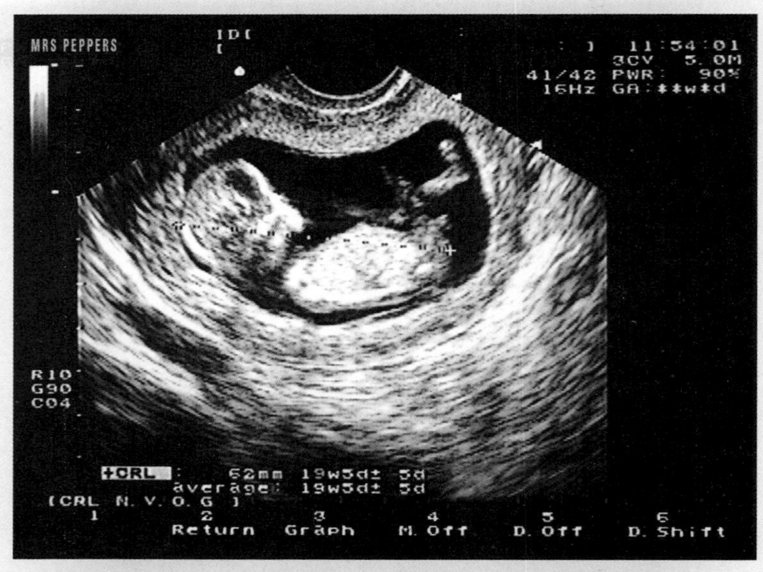

that we can't do it by ourselves. Our hearts are unclean and full of selfishness. We want God to forgive us and to make our hearts clean. We want so much to be good. We want to be like Jesus, but how can we?

You need rest for your bothered, sad heart. You need to know that Jesus forgives you. How can you have that rest in your heart? You can't buy it. You can't get it by thinking really hard. You can't even work to earn it!

Guess what? God wants to *give* you a happy, restful heart as a present! All you have to do is decide to take it.

Jesus says, "Even though your badness is as dark as the color of blood, it can be clean like fresh snow. Even though your sins are dirty, you can be clean like new white paper" (Isaiah 1:18).

God promises to give you a brand-new heart.

You have already told God that you are sorry for the times you've been bad. You've already chosen to put the bad things away. Now talk to Jesus and ask Him to wash away your sins and give you a new, clean heart. Then you can know He has done it, because He promised He would!

Jesus has taught us that when we believe that we will get a new heart, we will. In the Bible days, He was able to help people when they decided to believe He could. He loved to heal people's sick bodies so they would know that He could fix their sick hearts. If you want help to believe that Jesus will take away your sins, just spend time thinking about all the people in the Bible that He healed. Remember, He did this to make them healthy *and* holy.

Once, there was a man who lived at Bethesda. This man hurt and suffered all the time. He couldn't walk or even use his arms. But Jesus told him to pick up his blankets and walk. That sick man could have said, "Well, You see, I can't walk. But if You will fix my legs and arms, then I will obey You." But he didn't. He believed

Jesus, and Jesus made him strong to do what he was told. Jesus made him well!

We are sinners—we do bad things and break God's rules. We can't fix our own hearts and suddenly be good. But God promises to fix us! We believe Him. We say we are sorry for the bad things we have done and that we choose to give our hearts to Jesus. We *choose* to obey. Just as soon as we do this, God will make us strong to obey. We can believe that God gives us a new heart, and He really will! Jesus will give us new hearts, just like He gave that poor man a healed body.

Don't wait until you are holy and clean. Just say, "I believe it! I know it's really true because God promised me a brand-new heart!"

We can let Jesus give us a fresh heart. Then, when we pray and really believe, He'll give us many wonderful things. He wants us to be clean from sin and to be very good and holy. When we pray for these things, we can be sure that they will come true. Then we will never have to be embarrassed about who we are, because we are following Jesus.

God Is Your Helper

After supper David and Mr. Peppers were sitting on the couch, looking at the ultrasound pictures. They were having fun trying to figure out the baby's different body parts. In one picture, they could see the bones in the baby's back very clearly, and in another, they thought the baby was sucking his thumb. They laughed about how big his head was, and then they came to the picture of the baby's heart again.

"Mom," David asked, "do you have any more stories about a new heart? I want to hear more."

This time Christy ran to the shelf and grabbed the book. Mrs. Peppers slowly sat down beside the family.

From now on, you belong to Jesus. He bought you forever by dying for you. You believe in Jesus, and so now you have a brand-new heart. You are like a new baby Christian, and God loves you more than you know.

Now that you've given your heart to Jesus, don't change your mind. Every day you must choose to say, "I belong to Jesus because I gave my heart to Him." Pray that God's Holy Spirit will make you strong to be like Jesus. Just like you choose to give your heart to Jesus, you can choose to keep living for Him too.

Jesus wants to bless you with a happy heart right now. You must always remember that Jesus will help you get rid of the bad things in your life. Jesus knows just how naughty you are, but He loves to have you come to Him just the way you are. Go to Jesus. Pray to Him and be sad for how bad you've been. His goodness will wrap around you like a big hug, and He will make everything just right.

Some people don't believe that Jesus really wants to forgive them. But you can *know* that God will forgive you. Do you sometimes think that God doesn't want to forgive you? Don't even think about such a thing! No one is so bad that Jesus can't help him or her. Jesus is ready to take away from your heart everything that is ugly or dirty. He is ready to cover you with His wonderful sweetness.

Sometimes people have a hard time forgiving each other, but God is not like that. He is so kind to people. He says that just as soon as you throw away your sin and come back to Him, He will forgive you.

God knows that if we love to do bad things, someday we will die forever. But He loves us and doesn't want for us to die! Satan wants us to feel sad. He wants us to think that we *have* to die. Don't let him win! Don't ever listen to him. When Satan makes you think that you'll always be bad or that you will die forever, put your fingers in your ears and say, "Jesus died for me! He loves me and wants me to live forever. I *have* been bad, but God has kind heart and will help me again." God *will* help you.

God loves you so much. He loves you with a love that lasts forever, and His heart is full of kindness for you. If you feel that you want to love God and be near Him, it's because His Holy Spirit is in your heart, pulling you to God.

God has given you so many good promises; you don't need to worry at all. Don't ever think that God doesn't like to help you and forgive you. Don't think that God is mean—that just hurts your own heart.

Believe and Receive

Are you afraid that God doesn't like you? Look up to Jesus in heaven! He is your wonderful Helper. Be thankful, because Jesus died for you. Pray that God will help you to be good for Him. If you give your heart to Jesus, He will bless you and make you happy and good.

Remember, God's promises are in the Bible to tell us just how much He loves us. Jesus thinks about us and loves us with His whole heart. He will save us and forgive us when we do bad things.

God is our best Helper. He wants to make us good and sweet like He is. If we go to Jesus and tell Him that we are sorry when we disobey, He will come near us and forgive us.

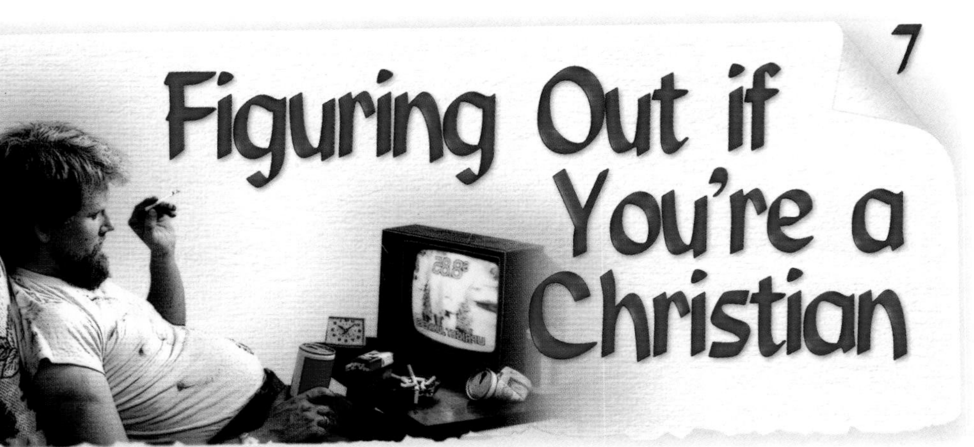

7 Figuring Out if You're a Christian

Different From the Way You Used to Be

It was morning and everyone wanted a story, so Mrs. Peppers said, "You know William's dad, Mr. Stanley?"

The children nodded. He was their favorite babysitter.

"Well, his wife told me something about him. Did you know that he used to say rude, mean things to her all the time?"

David was surprised that Mom would say such a thing about their friend. "Really?"

"Yes, David. And he used to spend hours every day watching TV and wasting his time on video games."

"He plays with us!" said Christy.

"Yes, now he spends his extra time playing with William and sometimes with you, too, doesn't he? He also used to get mad easily, but now he gets quiet when something upsets him, and he forgets about it quickly.

"He also used to spend money on drinking and other bad things. And his wife says that he smoked so much that he made the house stink. But now he saves that money and puts it in the offering at church every week. He even preaches now!

"That was just three years ago. How do you think he changed and became so different so quickly? He seems happy now."

Christy grinned and ran to the refrigerator. She pulled down the ultrasound pictures and hurried back. "A new heart!" she exclaimed, pointing to the picture of the baby's heart.

Mom smiled. "Yes, you're right." She opened up the book and pulled Christy onto her lap.

"If you belong to Jesus, you will be a brand-new person! Your life is no longer like it used to be. Everything is fresh and new" (2 Corinthians 5:17).

You may not remember just when or where you gave your heart to Jesus. That's OK. God's Spirit is still working on your heart. God is strong, and He knows just how to make your heart brand-new and lovely. Do you want to be like Jesus? He is strong enough to make you that way.

DAVID ASKS WHY

How do you know if you have a brand-new heart? You can't do anything special yourself to get a new heart. There's nothing you can do by yourself to become God's friend. You can't trust yourself, but you can trust Jesus.

When you have a new heart, people will notice that you are different from the way you used to be. You act differently and talk differently. You want to do different things. People will be able to tell that you are not like you used to be. People will know that you are a Christian by the things you usually do and say. Jesus will help you make good habits.

Do you know that some people have an unclean heart, but still act OK on the outside? These people do lots of good things so other people will like them or so their lives will be easier. Sometimes selfish people share. Sometimes people are very careful not to do anything mean just so they won't embarrass themselves.

So, if people who aren't really Christians can do good things, how can we know if we are Christians?

Here's how. Ask yourselves, Who has control of your heart? Who do you think about and talk about? Do you really love Jesus and want to obey Him? If you belong to Jesus, you will think about Him and be happy to give gifts to Him. You will want to be like Him and act like Him and be near Him. You will want to make Him happy.

When Jesus gives us new hearts, we will learn to be loving and cheerful and to have a restful heart and be patient. We will learn to be good and to believe in Jesus and not to be selfish. We will even learn to eat and play and work in just the right way—not too much and not too little! We will learn to be like Jesus. We will love the things we used to hate and hate the things we used to love. We will learn to let other people be first, and if we were loud and naughty before, now we will be calm and polite. A true Christian will learn to not worry about fancy clothes and toys. He or she will learn that the most beautiful person is the one who is sweet and kind.

People don't have changed hearts unless they act differently from the way they did before. If you have a new heart, it's time to make things right, to say you're sorry, to love everybody. Then you can know that God has changed your heart.

Promises and Being Good

"David! Come here! Will you please sweep the kitchen floor?"

"Aw, Mom! I don't want to. That's a hard job. I don't like it. *You* do it; you don't mind sweeping!"

Mom just laughed. "Well, I'd rather be doing something else, but *I* don't have to get grumpy."

David turned toward his mother, "What?"

She smiled handed him the broom and dustpan. Then she walked away, calling over her shoulder, "I have a secret weapon!"

David knew she meant business, so he swept the kitchen as fast as he could and then ran into the other room where Mrs. Peppers and Christy were just opening the book.

When sad, disobedient people come to Jesus and get a new heart, God puts love in their hearts. Every job they have is easier now. Whenever we give up something because Jesus asks us to, we can feel good. If life seemed sad and dark before, now it's all lit up with Jesus' happiness.

Jesus was so lovely and kind when He was here on earth. Those who follow Him will be that way too. Jesus loved to do whatever His Father asked Him to do. Jesus was excited about showing His love and about obeying His Father, and that's what helped Him to be strong to obey. Everything He did was sweet and kind because He loved people.

Love comes from God. A heart that doesn't belong to Jesus can't come up with love all by itself. The heart that belongs to Jesus is filled with true love. "We know how to love because God taught us how" (1 John 4:19). When we have new hearts, we will want to share God's love. God's love will change our hearts. It changes what we feel and think. This love makes our lives sweet and helps us make other people happy.

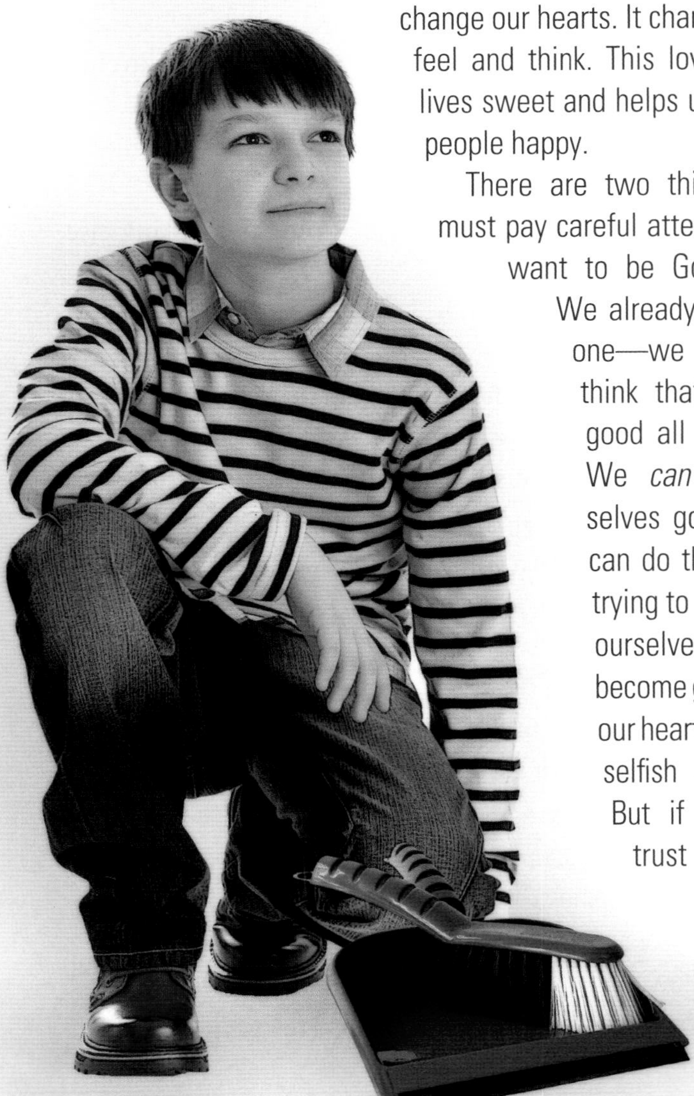

There are two things that we must pay careful attention to if we want to be God's children. We already talked about one—we must never think that we can be good all by ourselves. We *can't* make ourselves good; only God can do that. If we are trying to be good all by ourselves, we'll never become good, because our hearts are naturally selfish and naughty. But if we learn to trust in Jesus, He will make us good!

Figuring Out if You're a Christian

The other thing that we need to watch out for is this: some people think that God really doesn't care very much whether or not they obey Him. They think that because they believe in Jesus, they can do whatever they want!

We shouldn't obey just because we think God *makes* us obey. We should obey because we love God. When we love Him, we'll do what He asks us to. God's rules teach us how to be like Him. And when we love Him, we will learn to keep His law. When we learn to keep His law, we are learning to be loving just like He is.

If you listen closely at church, you may hear people talking about something called "the new covenant." A covenant is a very special promise that people make to each other. God promises to save you and make you just like Him. That is the new covenant. He says that He will write His rules in your heart. That means that you will *want* to do what God asks you to do. And He will help you. It will change almost everything you do.

Do you want to be God's helper? You can be when you obey Him. The Bible says that when we really love God, we will obey Him. If we say we love God, but don't do what He tells us to, we are liars. When we believe in God and when we love Him, it doesn't mean we can do whatever we want. It means He will make us strong to do what *He* wants us to do.

Remember, God doesn't save you because you are good. He saves you because it's His special gift to you. But when you get that gift, you will learn to obey. The Bible says that if you keep Jesus close to you all day long, you don't have to sin or do bad things anymore. If you stay with Jesus, you will feel better. You will think good thoughts, and you will be nice to other people. Don't let anyone fool you. People who are holy and good will keep God's rules. But if they keep on breaking God's rules, they are not holy.

If you say that you believe in God, but you decide to do what you want to do instead of obeying God, you are not really a Christian. One time, Jesus said to God, His Father, "I love to do whatever You ask Me to do. I like to obey Your laws" (Psalm 40:8). Just before He went back to heaven, Jesus said, "I have obeyed all of My Father's commandments; I live every day in His love" (John 15:10). Do you know how you can tell if someone is a Christian? If they live like Jesus lived and do the kind of things He did, they are a Christian (1 John 2:3–6; 1 Peter 2:21).

God's rules for living forever with Him are the same as they always have been. We must obey all of God's laws. We must be like Jesus. If God let everyone—even mean, wicked people—live forever and ever, no one could be happy. God just can't let badness go on forever and ever.

When God made the first man, Adam, he was perfect. He was able to be good and holy all by himself. But he chose to sin. Since then, people just can't be good all by themselves. We are sinful—we aren't good at all. God's law expects certain things from us, and we don't have anything inside of us that can make us do what we need to do. But God planned a way for us to escape. The plan was this: He would live here on earth as a man. He had some really hard times and was tempted just like we are. Yet He never sinned—not even once! Then He died for us. Now He has offered to trade places with us. He will take away our sins and give us His goodness and holiness. Even though we have been bad before, if we give ourselves completely to Jesus, He will treat us just like we have never sinned. Jesus' goodness takes the place of our badness, and God accepts us as His children—just as though we were never bad at all.

In fact, God tells everyone that we are holy, but He does more than that. He changes our hearts by moving in and making them His home. When we choose to really believe in God, He will come and live in our hearts. But we have to keep letting Him stay there. If we choose to obey everything God asks us to do, He will stay in our hearts. As long as we choose to believe and obey, He will make us strong to do everything He has asked us to do. Then we can say, "I live my life by believing in Jesus because He loves me and died for me!" (Galatians 2:20). Once Jesus moves into our hearts, we will be like Him. We will act like Him and obey and do the kinds of things that He would do.

There's nothing about us that's worth bragging about. We shouldn't try to make other people think that we are important. But we can know that everything will be OK when Jesus says we're OK and when His Holy Spirit does wonderful things in us.

Busy Faith

After church David and Christy were waiting for Dad to finish making the salad while Mom sat down and propped up her tired feet. They started singing a new song they had learned in class that morning. It was a silly song about Pharisees, Sadducees, and sheep. Dad smiled at his wife. "There's your favorite song, honey."

"Ugh! You know I don't like that song. People always sing it over and over and over and—"

"All right! We know!" Dad interrupted, laughing.

"I tell you what, kids," Mom said, "if you'll come rub my feet, I'll tell you all about Pharisees and Sadducees."

Christy grabbed the lotion, but David rolled his eyes. "Aw, Mom, not your feet!"

"Well," Mom grinned, "if you're not willing to pay the price."

David laughed and took the lotion from Christy. He squirted too much into his open hand and sat down. He started rubbing Mom's foot.

"The song says that Sadducees are 'sad.' That's because of what they believed. They said that God loves us already and that we can't do anything to change that. So they didn't worry about keeping any rules—not even God's rules. Well, you know no one likes people who don't keep rules, so not very many people liked Sadducees."

"I know some people who don't like rules," Dad called from the kitchen.

"Me?" asked David.

"Shh!" said Mom. "Pharisees really liked rules. They read that God's law is important, so they made up lots of extra rules. They wanted to make sure that everyone kept God's law just the way they thought it should be kept. But their rules weren't fair, and no one really liked them either. So, who was right? Should we keep God's rules?"

"Yes!" shouted David.

"No!" Christy shook her head.

Mom picked up the book and started to read.

When you talk about faith, there's something you should always remember. You may believe something, but it may not really be faith at all. Even Satan knows that there is a God and that He is very strong. Satan and his angels even know that the Bible is really true—but that's not the same as having faith in God or in the Bible. Faith is believing what God says and obeying; it's giving your heart to Him and loving Him. That's faith. Faith is busy too. Faith makes you love, and it makes you do nice things. It makes your heart clean and beautiful. When God first made people, they were a lot like Him. When you have faith, you begin to look and act and be like God.

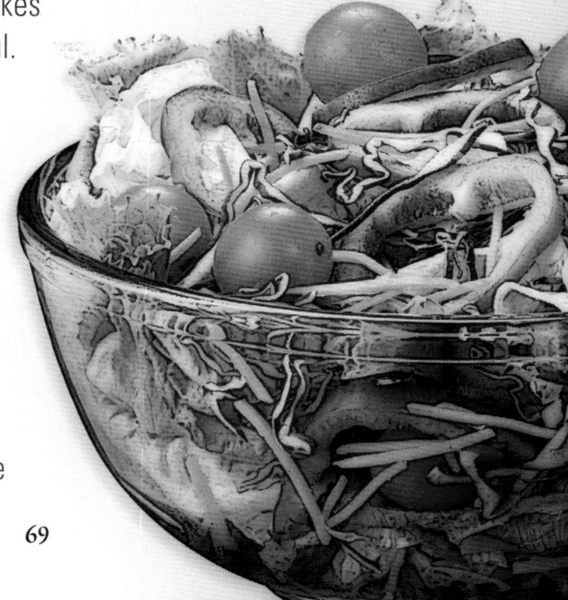

Before someone gives his or her heart to God and He makes it new, that person can't keep God's law. But afterward, the same person loves to obey God's law! King David told God, "I love Your law! I think about it all the time" (Psalm 119:97). You'll feel the same way when you give your heart to Jesus. And when you follow God's Holy Spirit, you will be able to do what He wants you to do.

Some people really want to be God's children. God has forgiven them, and they know that He loves them. But they also know that they aren't perfect and that they have problems. They wonder if maybe they are not really Christians after all. Is that how you feel? Well, don't stop now! Many times you will make mistakes. When this happens, don't be sad! Even if Satan trips you up and tricks you into being bad, Jesus won't push you away. God the Father is in heaven, and Jesus is right beside Him, telling His Father all about how much He loves you.

Jesus' good friend, the disciple John, said, "I'm telling you these things so that you don't sin. But if one of you does sin, don't forget that Jesus, who is perfect, is your Friend, and He is on your side" (1 John 2:1). And don't forget Jesus said that His Father loves you very much (John 16:27). He wants to bring you back to be close to Him. He wants you to have His own pure goodness shining out of you. He has already started doing wonderful things in your heart, and if you choose to obey Him, He'll help you more and more until He comes. Pray and really, truly believe. When you learn that you can't trust yourself, then you'll be able to trust Jesus all the way. Then you'll sing songs of praise to the God who gives you a happy look on your face.

The more we get to know Jesus, the more we will see how much we need Him. We will see how much better He is than we are. This is a good thing, because it means that Satan's lies aren't working so well anymore. Jesus is waking up our hearts and making us grow!

Figuring Out if You're a Christian

When we really learn to love Jesus, we'll be able to see that our hearts are actually naughty. But Jesus will change our hearts, and we will love Him more and more. If we don't see how much we need Jesus, it's because we don't know how wonderful He is.

When we learn that there is nothing good about ourselves, then we can see how really great Jesus is. Then we will go to Him to be forgiven. He will show us how strong He is. We must learn how much we need Jesus, and then we will want to pray and read the Bible. When we do this, we'll see how awesome Jesus is, and we will become more like Him.

Grow Like a Tree

Such a beautiful new baby! Little Daniel was perfect. David especially loved to hold him and watch him and sing to him. But after a few weeks, he wasn't so sure about how much fun a baby brother was going to be. He pulled on Daniel's fat legs and ran them like a bike, but though the baby laughed, nothing else happened. David wanted Daniel to grow so he could play and walk and have fun with him. But he just lay there, and it was kind of boring.

Mom said they'd have to wait a while, but that reminded her of today's story, and so she pulled out the book and began to read.

When Jesus gives us a new heart, we become God's children. This is what the Bible calls "being born again." The Bible says that this is also like a new little plant that sprouts from a seed. When people become Jesus' new children, they are like newborn babies, and then they grow up to be Jesus' men and women

(1 Peter 2:2; Ephesians 4:15). Just like a seed that is planted in the ground, new Christians will grow fruit. The good things that fill up the Christians' lives are like fruit. Isaiah says that Christians are like good trees that God has planted. And the good fruit they grow helps people to see how wonderful God really is (Isaiah 61:3). When we see the things God makes and learn from them, it helps us understand what it means to be a Christian.

People can work and work and try and try, but they can never make something alive. Only God knows how to make something alive. In the same way, only God can give you a brand-new heart and make you "born again." Unless you are born again in this way, you can never have the life that Jesus came to give you.

Growing works the same way that living does. God is the One who makes flowers bloom and plants grow fruit. God is the One who makes a little seed turn into a sprout and then a piece of fruit, and then ripe fruit (Mark 4:28). Prophet Hosea in the Bible says that God's people will grow like the flowers, the corn, and the grapevine (Hosea 14:5, 7).

Jesus tells us to think about how the lilies grow (Luke 12:27). Plants and flowers don't worry or fuss or try really hard to grow. They just take all the good things God sends to give them life. A little child can't make himself taller just by worrying and trying. You can't make yourself grow to be like Jesus by worrying or trying either! The plant and the little child grow because they take in all the things around them that give life—things like fresh air and sunshine and good food. For Christians, Jesus is like fresh air and sunshine and food that cause us to grow and become like Him.

Jesus is like a light that lasts forever—He's like the sun. He's also our Protector and loves to take care of us (Isaiah 60:19; Psalm 84:11). The Bible says He's like water to drink and bread to eat. When we soak Him up and take Him in, He gives us life (Hosea 14:5; Psalm 72:6; John 6:33).

There is air all around the world, and Jesus' saving love is kind of like that—it's everywhere. Everyone who wants to can breathe in this love and power, and it will make them grow up to be God's men and women.

When flowers are growing, they turn their faces toward the sun. This helps them grow and be more beautiful and perfect. The Bible calls Jesus the Sunshine of goodness; and if we look to Him, His light will shine on us. Then we'll grow and grow and become like Him.

Jesus teaches us the same thing. He said, "Stay close to Me and let Me stay close to you. A branch on a tree can't make any fruit unless it's connected to the tree, and you can't make any fruit unless you stick with Me. You can't do anything without Me" (John 15:4, 5). If a branch is broken off the vine that grew it, it will die. And if you go away from Jesus, you can't have live a holy, good life either. You can't grow, and you can't say No to Satan if you don't let Jesus stay in your heart. As long as you keep getting life from Jesus, you will be fresh and lovely, and your life will be full of good things. You'll be strong and lovely, kind of like the beautiful green trees that grow by the water.

Sticking With Jesus

Mrs. Peppers was feeling better these days. Little Daniel was here, and she was feeling stronger. One day while Daniel was sleeping, Mrs. Peppers stood in the doorway and watched David and Christy playing quietly. She knew that they wanted to be like Jesus. She had a good idea.

Later, when Mr. Peppers came home, she asked him to stay with the children while she went out for a while. She was gone for a long time, so Dad put David and Christy to bed. When Mom got home, she came in with two bags and went to her room. It was a long time before she went to bed.

The next morning, David and Christy were up early and ran into their parents' room. "Are you awake?" they asked as they came through the door.

Dad was studying at his desk. He spun around in his chair. "*Shh!* Your mom was up late. Let her sleep."

But Mom rolled over and smiled. "Good morning! Go to the living room, and I'll be there in a minute."

A few minutes later, Mom came into the living room in her pretty purple robe. She had her hands behind her back. "Come sit down. I have a surprise for you."

David and Christy sat down, and Mom put a pretty present in front of each of them.

"Open them."

They tore them open quickly. Christy wasn't sure what to do with the tiny CD player.

Mom showed Christy and David how to put the CD into the player and how to connect the headphones.

"Now each of you can spend time getting to know Jesus all by yourself whenever you want. I hope you will listen at least every morning. I'll help you remember."

They turned on their new gifts and heard Mom reading.

Many people think if they trust Jesus, He will forgive them. But they also think that if they want to be a Christian, they have to work really hard to be good. You can try and try by yourself—but it just won't work! Jesus said you can't do anything without Him. If you want to grow in Jesus, if you want to be happy and a good helper, you have to count on Jesus. If you stick close to Him, if you spend time with Him and talk to Him always, every day, you will grow. The Bible calls this "abiding in Him." Jesus is the One who helped us believe on Him, and He is the One who will make us perfect and lovely. Jesus is the most important thing—first, last, and always. He promises to be with you every moment of every day. King David said that he paid attention to the Lord all the time. He knew that because Jesus was with Him all the time, no one could ever make Him do wrong (Psalm 16:8).

Do you wonder how you're supposed to stay with Jesus? The Bible says, "Walk in Jesus the same way that you let Him come into to your heart in the first place" (Colossians 2:6). If you want to be good and holy, you must truly believe in Jesus (Hebrews 10:38). You gave your heart and your life to Jesus so that you could be all His. You want to obey Him and make Him happy because you know He is the One who saves you. You could never make your sins go away or get a new heart by yourself, but you know that God did this

for you. You chose to believe and give your heart to Jesus. You will grow in the same way. Choose to keep giving your heart to Jesus and taking the wonderful gifts He has for you.

Keep giving everything to Jesus. Choose to love Him and obey Him in everything He asks.

Then you must take everything He wants to give you. He wants to give you Himself and to be your Friend. He will give you a happy heart. He will live inside your heart and make you be strong and good. He will help forever and make you strong to obey.

When you first wake up in the morning, promise your heart to God. Pray to Jesus, "Make me all Yours, dear Lord. I want You to be the Boss of my day. Let me be a helper for You today. Stay with me and help me do what You want me to do." You need to do this every day. Every morning you must give your whole day to God. Let Him teach you what to do that day. Let Him help you choose what to do all day long. Every day you can give your life to God again, and then you will become more and more like Jesus.

If you want to have rest in your heart and not have to worry, you can just keep giving your life to Jesus. You may not feel excited, but you can trust Jesus. You don't have to believe in yourself and just hope that you can do what you need to do. You can just believe in Jesus Christ.

You are really weak by yourself, but you and Jesus can be a team. He's strong and you are weak. He is smart and you don't know very much. You don't have to worry about being a Christian all by yourself. Don't even think about yourself—think about Jesus. Think about His love and beauty and goodness. Jesus put other people first and was humble. He was pure and holy. Think about the best love that ever was—Jesus' love.

Do you want to be like Jesus? Here's how. You must love Him and copy Him. You must count on Him to help you, and you will become like Him.

Jesus tells us, "Abide in Me." This teaches us rest and trust. We don't have to always change our minds or become confused. Jesus helps us to know what we have to do. He says, "If you come to Me, I will give you rest" (Matthew 11:28). King David says the same thing. "Rest in God, and wait for Him patiently" (Psalm 37:7). The prophet Isaiah tells us that we can be strong when we're quiet and sure in God (Isaiah 30:15). Now, we're not talking about being lazy. Jesus said that we can have peaceful hearts of rest only when we work with Him. He says that if we work with Him, that He will give us quiet, peaceful hearts (Matthew 11:29). We can rest the best when we've worked the hardest for Jesus.

It's Not About You

One morning the family decided to read the book of Psalms together. Dad always liked to change the words a little, so he read the verses like this:

The person who ignores the advice of people who don't love God will be really happy. He'll be happy if he doesn't do the things that sinners do or mock people. This kind of person loves God's law—it makes him happy because he thinks about it all the time.

This kind of person is like a tree planted near a river—a tree that has plenty of water and produces a lot of fruit and has beautiful green leaves all year long. Everything this person does will turn out well.

A person who doesn't love God won't be able to make it through the hard times ahead. When God judges that person, He'll take the good person's side. The Lord knows just what the good person's life will be like. He knows that the wicked person will end up dead (Psalm 1:1–6).

"You know," said Dad, "if we spend our time thinking about Jesus and the Bible, we can be happy. Some people are scared of what will happen to this world, but we don't have to be afraid if we keep Jesus in our hearts."

Then Mom opened the book and began to read.

When you think about yourself, you can't really spend time thinking about Jesus. But He's the only way to be strong and have a real life. This is why Satan tries and tries to take your thoughts away from Jesus. He doesn't want you to be friends with Jesus. Satan likes for you to think about how much fun you can have doing just what you want to do. He wants you to think about all the worries and sadness going on everywhere. He loves for you to think about how bad someone else is or maybe even how bad you are. Don't be tricked by his lies! If you want to follow Jesus, Satan will try to get you to worry about how bad and weak you are. This is how he wants to take your heart away from Jesus.

Stop thinking so much about yourself! You don't have to be scared and wonder if Jesus will save you. This just makes you forget Jesus and how strong He is. Trust God with your heart. Talk about Jesus and think about Him. Start thinking about Jesus instead of yourself. Don't be scared. Don't do your own thing anymore, but let Jesus make your choices for you. Trust in Him because He loves you so much that He died for you (Galatians 2:20). If you let Jesus help you, He will make you a real winner because He loves you so much!

When Jesus became a person like us, He tied Himself to us by love. Nothing can ever take us away from Jesus unless we choose to push Him away. Satan always brings exciting things to tempt us to push Jesus away. This is why we need to pay attention and pray and do our best so that nothing will make us choose Satan instead of Jesus. We can choose to follow Satan or Jesus—either one. But keep looking at Jesus, and He will keep you strong. As long as you keep looking at Jesus, you are safe. Nothing can take you away from Him. As you watch Him and learn about Him, you will "be made more and more like Him, because His Holy Spirit will help you" (2 Corinthians 3:18).

This is how Jesus' special friends, the disciples, became so much like their dear Jesus. When they heard Jesus talking, they knew that they needed Him. They looked for Him and found Him, and then they followed Him. They stayed with Him all the time—while they slept and ate and prayed and walked outside. Every day, they learned from Jesus, their Teacher. Every day, He taught them new lessons about God's truth. They paid attention to Jesus? because they wanted to be His servants and to learn how to obey Him. The disciples had the same feelings we have; they had hard times, just as we do (James 5:17). They were tempted to sin, and they needed Jesus so that they could live good lives.

John called himself the disciple that Jesus loved. He was the most like Jesus of all the disciples, but he wasn't this way on his own. On his own, he was selfish and wanted people to think he was important. He was rude and became hateful when people were mean to him. But as He watched Jesus and saw how good He was, he saw how weak he, himself, was. He watched how strong and patient Jesus was. Jesus was strong, but kind and gentle. He was like a king, but He was also humble and not selfish. Every day, John watched these things in Jesus, and he learned to love Jesus and to want to be just like Him. Every day, he learned to love Jesus more until he didn't even think about himself anymore. All he could think about was his love for Jesus. Jesus' power changed John's bad temper. The Holy Spirit gave him a brand-new heart. Jesus' love was so strong that it changed John's whole life. And this is what always happens when we become friends with Jesus. When Jesus lives in our hearts and changes us, He gives us better thoughts and helps us love God and heaven.

God's Holy Spirit

One day David was playing with the other children in school when someone offered him a snack that he'd never had before. He said, "No, thank you," but the other children tried to get him to eat it. Even his teacher wanted him to take some, but he knew his mom wouldn't want him to.

Later Tommy told him, "I just love that stuff! I know it's not good for you, but it's not *that* bad. How could you say No?"

"I don't know. I just didn't think I should eat it."

Later, at home, David asked, "Dad, why did I say No? I didn't even mean to. I wanted some, but I just couldn't."

Dad smiled and gave him a hug. "Let's go see if your mom will read to us. I think you'll find the answer to your question in what she will read from the book."

When they found her, Mrs. Peppers was glad to read further.

Even after Jesus went back up to heaven, the people who loved Him still felt that He was near them in their hearts. They felt that He was really still there with them, and they could still feel His love. Jesus was the One who'd saved them. He had walked with them and talked and prayed with them. He had given them hope and had made their hearts happy. As He was going back to heaven, His words had come back to them: "Listen," He said, "I will be with you always. I will be with you even to the very end of the world" (Matthew 28:20).

Jesus had gone back up to heaven. His friends knew that now He was beside His Father's throne, but that He was still their Friend. They knew He still loved. Jesus showed His Father the good work that He had done on earth. He showed Him the scars in His hands and feet that He got from dying for people on earth. His friends were happy because they knew He'd gone to heaven to get things ready for them and that He'd come back and get them.

After Jesus went back to heaven, His friends were excited to get together for prayer meetings. Now they prayed to God in Jesus' name. They remembered that Jesus had said, "If you ask the Father for anything in My name, He will give it to you. You haven't asked anything in My name yet, but when you do, you'll get what you ask for. And you can be completely happy" (John 16:23, 24).

They trusted Jesus more and more because they knew that He had died for them and that He had come to life again and was with God the Father. He knew He was their Friend (Romans 8:34).

Jesus had promised them that after He left, Someone else would come to live inside their hearts. He said that for Him to go back to heaven was actually the best thing for them, because then they could have this new Friend (John 16:23, 24). This new Friend, the Holy Spirit, came just fifty days after Jesus rose up from the dead. This is how Jesus was able to stay in the hearts of His friends all the time. Now they could be even closer and better friends with Him than they ever had been before.

Jesus' friends were full of His love and power and truth. Other people saw them and were surprised and paid attention to them, because the people could tell that they'd been with Jesus (Acts 4:13).

Jesus wants to be your Friend and Helper just as He was to His special friends, the disciples. The last time that Jesus prayed with His friends, He said, "I'm not praying just for these people here, but I'm praying for everyone who will ever believe on Me" (John 17:20).

Jesus was praying for us! He asked His Father to draw us so close to Him that we would be like one person with Him. This is just the way that Jesus and His Father are, and He wants to be that close to us too. What a wonderful friendship! Jesus said that He couldn't do anything by Himself. He said that His Father lived in His heart and that His Father was the One who did things for Him (John 5:19; 14:10).

So, if we let Jesus live in our hearts, He will help us do good things (Philippians 2:13). We will work like He worked, and we will have the same attitude He had. When we love Jesus and stay with Him, we will grow up to be just like Him (Ephesians 4:15).

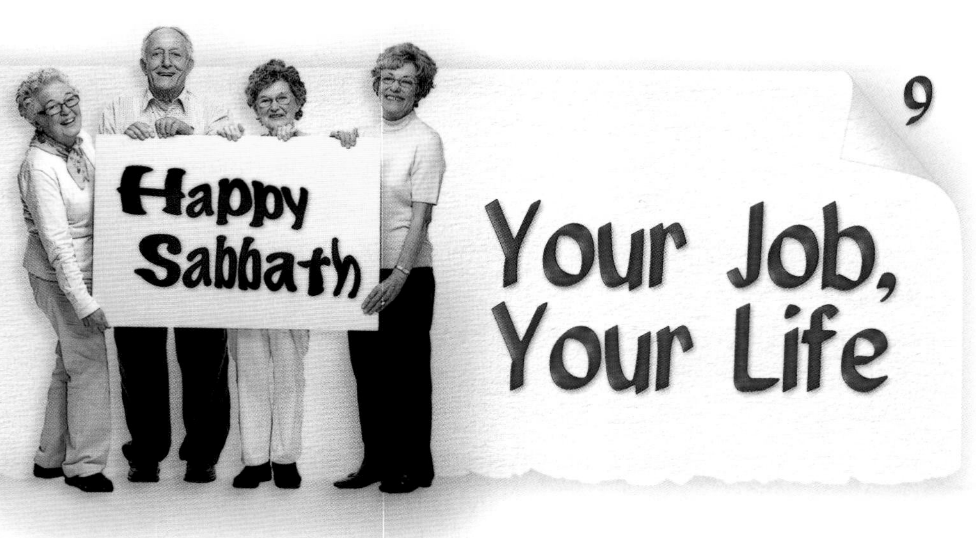

9 Your Job, Your Life

You Can Be a Present to Someone Else

The pastor invited some friends to go to a church service at a nursing home one Sabbath afternoon. Mrs. Peppers and David went to help; they sang a song together. It was a fun song, and the old people really loved it.

Before they left, they shook the old men's hands and let the old women kiss them on their cheeks. On the way home, they talked about how much fun they had had, and when they came inside, David got their book. Mom brought Daniel in to feed him, and Christy came in, rubbing her eyes from a nap.

Life and light and happiness come from God. He shares these things with everyone and everything He made. If people have God's life in their hearts, they will share that with other people the same way God shares good things with them. They will share love and good things to others.

More than anything else, Jesus loved to lift up people and save them. He was even willing to die, if He could just save people. That is why He died on the cross. God's angels spend all of their time working to make other people happy too. That is what angels most love to do. Selfish people think it's embarrassing to help people who are less important than they are. But angels like to do it.

Jesus isn't selfish at all. He always puts other people first. So does everyone in heaven. That's why heaven is such a happy place. People here on earth who really love Jesus will be this way too. They will do what needs to be done to help and care for other people.

When Jesus' love is in your heart, it will be so sweet that you can't hide it. That love is holy, and everyone who comes near will feel it. When Jesus is in your heart, you'll be like water to thirsty people who feel they are going to die without a drink of water. They will be thirsty to know that Jesus loves them.

If you love Jesus, you will want to help people the way He did. His love will make you loving and gentle. It will make you kind to every person or animal that God has made.

Jesus wasn't lazy. He didn't spend His time trying to make Himself more comfortable. He worked hard to save people. From the time He was born until the time He died, He was never selfish. He didn't try to get out of doing hard jobs or long, tiring trips or hard work. He said, "I didn't come so you could help Me. I came to help people and then to die for them" (Matthew 20:28).

The main thing Jesus came to do was to help people. Nothing else was quite so important to Him. The things He did were never selfish.

If you have Jesus' love and power in your life, you'll be willing to give up anything so that other people can go to heaven with you. You will do all you can to make the world better. That's how people are who have new hearts. As soon as you come to Jesus, you'll want to tell other people about your precious Friend. You can't hide the fact that He's your Helper. If Jesus' righteousness is covering you like a warm, beautiful coat, if you have God's Holy Spirit in your heart, you won't be able to keep quiet about it! If you have learned how good Jesus is, you will just have to tell other people. You'll want to invite them to come meet Jesus too. You will want to tell them about your wonderful Jesus and about heaven. You will want to follow Jesus and be just like Him. You'll want other people to meet Jesus who can take away their sins (John 1:29)!

And when you try to bless other people and make them happy, it will make you happy too. That's why God wants us to help Him save people, because when we tell someone about Him, it makes us really, truly happy. When we take the new heart that Jesus wants to give us, then it will be our turn to share what we have with other people. The most important job we can ever have—and the thing that will make us most happy—is to share God's good things with other people. If you want to become a very close friend with Jesus, work with Him because you love Him.

God could have asked angels to tell people about Him and His love. He could have had them do all the work. But He loved us so much that He let us work with Him and the angels. We get to share blessings and happiness with other people!

When someone hurts us or is mean to us, we understand how Jesus felt when people were mean to Him. Every time we give up something to help someone, we learn to love giving. This is how we learn to be part of Jesus' team—the team that helps Him save the world. The Bible says Jesus "used to be rich, but He decided to be poor so that we could be rich" (2 Corinthians 8:9). If you want to have a happy life, you give and share with others. Be unselfish, because that's what God wants.

When you work like Jesus wants you to and help people to know and love Him, you will understand that you need more and more of Jesus and His goodness yourself. Then you will pray, and God will give you more faith so that you will believe in Him even more. You will be filled with His goodness and power. When bad things happen or when people are mean, pray more and read the Bible. Then you will grow in Jesus' love and power, and you will know Him better and be happier.

God's Job for You

"Mom, can I make a card for Miss Jennings, the old woman we met at the nursing home?"

"Sure, David. Maybe we can take it to her tonight when Dad gets home."

David worked with glue and glitter and scissors all afternoon. When Mr. Peppers got home, David ran to him.

"Dad, look at my card! I made it for Miss Jennings."

"I packed a picnic supper," Mom told Dad. "I thought we could stop by the nursing home for a few minutes on our way to the park. Is that all right?"

"So you all have my whole evening planned for me! May I put on some comfortable clothes first?" Dad smiled.

After Mr. Peppers changed clothes, the family drove to the nursing home. When they went in, Miss Jennings was just finishing supper in her room. She was very happy to see David and Christy even though she wasn't feeling very well.

"I'm sorry you're sick, Miss Jennings! I made a card for you," David said, handing it to her.

The old woman smiled. "Thank you, dear!" She took the card from the envelope and looked at it through her thick glasses. She read what David had written, and then she even turned the card over to look at the back. "I think that is the nicest card I ever had," she told David.

They didn't stay long because they didn't want Miss Jennings to get too tired. But they sang and laughed as they got back into the car. They all felt happy because Miss Jennings was so happy.

When you are unselfish, like Jesus, you will be lovely like Jesus. You will be happy, and there will be no room in your life to be lazy or selfish. As you practice being this kind of a Christian, you'll grow and become a strong worker for God. You'll be able to better understand things about God, and your faith fill be stronger. Your prayers will be strong and powerful too. God's Spirit will change you and make you more and more lovely. If you spend your time learning to help others and not be selfish, you will show that Jesus has saved you.

There is only one way for God's love and power to grow in your life: Do the work Jesus wants you to do. Do the best job you can to help the people who need you. If you exercise, your body becomes stronger. To live a healthy, active life, you have to run and jump and play. It's the same with your love for God. If you just take all the gifts God gives you, and then sit back and be lazy and never do anything for Jesus, it's like never exercising your muscles. It doesn't work very well. If you don't do anything except eat and eat, you'll die. And if you just take all of God's gifts and don't share them with others, you'll wither away spiritually. You won't grow, and before long, you won't be a Christian at all!

Who do you think God expects to teach people how to have their sins forgiven and be saved? It's His church on earth—His people. The church's job is to tell people everywhere the good news about Jesus. This is what every Christian should be doing. We need to tell people about Jesus as best we can and teach them to love and follow Him. God gave us the wonderful things of love and heaven so that we could share them with everyone we meet.

We need to wake up and do what we're supposed to do. When we do, many people everywhere will be telling other people about Jesus, even though now there are just a few. You may not be able to go to some faraway country and tell people about Jesus, but you can give money to send people who *can* go. And you can be kind and helpful wherever you are—and pray for those who have gone far away to share Jesus' love. If we would wake up and do what we need to do, more people everywhere would know about Jesus.

We don't have to go to places that have never heard of Jesus. We can work for Jesus in our own house if that is where He wants us to work. We can share Jesus with our family and with people in our church. We should share Jesus with our friends and with the people in our neighborhood or at school or at the store.

When Jesus was here on earth, He spent most of His life working to build things as a carpenter. He lived and worked with poor people, and angels helped Him as He worked hard at the job He was suppose to do. For most of Jesus' life on earth, people didn't even know who He was, and it seemed that no one really cared. He was faithful though. He was just as good a worker as a carpenter at home as He was later when He healed people and preached. Whatever your job is, Jesus will help you, and when you do your job well, you are working with Him.

The Bible says, "Whatever you are supposed to do, stay close to God while you do it" (1 Corinthians 7:24). If people are really Christians, they will be Christians in every little thing they do, no matter what their jobs are. This is one way to show Jesus to other people. Christians are always good workers. When people see this, they will learn to love Jesus too.

Sometimes people say, "That person over there does a much better job than I do. I'll just let them do it all. I shouldn't waste my time." Should people who are really smart or good at what they do be the only ones who should work for God? Of course not! The Bible tells us to give what we have and share what we can. We must all do the very best job we can. Then when Jesus comes again, He will be happy and will pay attention to everything we've done.

Your Job, Your Life

When we have any work to do, we should do it with a loving heart, because we're really doing it for Jesus (Colossians 3:23). If we really love God, we'll act like it. The sweet fragrance of Jesus' love will be all around us, and other people will be lifted up and made happier, just because we're around.

Don't wait until you can do something big and special before you do anything for God. Don't worry about what other people think of you. If you are pure and sweet and if you believe in God and if other people know that you want to help them, then everything you do will be a help to someone.

Even if someone is ordinary or poor, he or she can still make other people happy. Sometimes we don't even know how much we are helping someone. We can't know all the good things that happen because we are kind and helpful—and we won't until Jesus comes again. We may not think our work is very special, but we don't have to worry about it. If we just keep on quietly doing what Jesus has asked us to do, we will be a really big help to many people. And all the time, our hearts will be growing more and more like Jesus' heart because when we work with God, it makes us ready for heaven.

Go Outside!

David put down his headphones and asked, "What's God like? I mean, what's He really like?"

Mr. and Mrs. Peppers were just finishing up some cleaning around the house. They smiled at each other.

"Let's go for a walk!" Dad suggested.

In a few minutes, Dad and Mom and David and Christy were headed out the door. Mom pushed Baby Daniel in his stroller.

"Look at that tree!" Mom pointed to the biggest tree on the street. "You see how huge it is? That's what God's like. He's big and strong, and He keeps us safe."

Dad pointed out a flower. "See the pretty little bud? There are beautiful things everywhere. God is beautiful, and He loves beautiful things. He wants to make your life beautiful too."

The family walked for more than an hour. They took turns pointing out things they saw and sharing what each thing told them about God. When they got home, they sat down together to read.

Knowing God

God teaches us about Himself in many different ways. He wants to be our special Friend and spend time with us. The things He made fill our eyes and ears and noses with wonderful things all the time. If our hearts are soft, we can see God's love and just how wonderful He is by looking at the things in nature that He has made.

Just go outside and see the green grass and the tall trees, the flowers, the clouds and the rain, the little streams of water, the big beautiful sky. All of these things talk to us in our hearts. They can help us know the God who made them.

Jesus told lots of interesting stories and lessons about such things as trees and birds and flowers and hills and lakes and skies. He told stories about all the little things that happen around us during the day. All these things have lessons to teach us about

God. These lessons are everywhere, so that even when we're busy, we can learn to think about the important things God wants to teach us.

God wants us to really enjoy the things He's made—the simple, quiet, beautiful things that are everywhere around us. God loves beautiful things, especially beautiful hearts. He wants us to be pure and sweet and simple just like the flowers.

If we will just listen, the things God has made will teach how to obey and how to trust Him. The stars obey God by going on and on in the path He tells them to follow. Even the very tiniest things that God made obey Him! God takes care of all the things He made. He holds up the big stars, and He takes care of the little brown birds, so they can sing and don't have to be scared.

When you work or pray, when you lie down to sleep, when you wake up in the morning, whether you have plenty to eat or just a little, your Father in heaven watches you carefully. He notices when you cry and when you smile.

If we really believed this, we wouldn't have to worry about foolish little things. We wouldn't have to be so sad when things don't go just the way we want, because God is taking care of it all. God isn't bothered by our little problems, He doesn't think they're too heavy to carry. If we trust in God, we can have rest in our hearts.

As you spend time looking at the beautiful things all around you, think about heaven and the new earth. In the new earth, there won't be anything bad to ruin its loveliness—and no one will ever die. Try to imagine just how wonderful our new home will be, and then remember that it will be even more wonderful than you can dream!

God has given us many lovely things in nature, but they show us just a little bit of what He's like. The Bible says, "No one has ever seen anything like it. No one has ever heard things so wonderful. No one can even imagine the wonderful things that God is getting ready for those who love Him" (1 Corinthians 2:9).

Artists paint pictures of the things God has made, and scientists know many facts about them. These are nice. But Christians like best the beautiful things themselves that God has made—because they know who made them! They know that every flower and bush and tree is just a nice present from God to us. If you want to know how wonderful the hills and valley and rivers and seas are, remember that God made them to tell you that He loves you.

Read Your Bible!

The next morning, Mr. Peppers read to David and Christy from the Bible. Afterward, as Dad was putting the Book away, David asked, "The Bible is another way we can learn about God, isn't it?"

"Of course!" Dad nodded. "In fact, it's just about the best way. We should read the Bible and memorize its words. That's a very good way to learn about God.

"I have to go to work now," he said, looking at his wife, "but I'll bet Mom would read to you if you go get your book."

God teaches in other ways than through nature. He teaches us through miracles and special feelings that He puts into our hearts. If we look at all the things that happen around us and pay attention, we can learn lessons. The Bible says that God's goodness is everywhere, and that if we are wise, we will watch and learn about how kind and loving God is (Psalms 33:5; 107:43).

God also teaches us from the Bible. This is where can really see what He is like and how He treats people. In the Bible, we can learn how God saves people. Here we find the stories of the people and prophets who loved God.

The Bible teaches us that the heroes in the Bible were a lot like us (James 5:17). They became frustrated and sad just as we do. Sometimes, like us, they disobeyed and sinned. But be-

cause Jesus loved them and promised to give them power, they were able to be strong and do what is right. If we spend time learning about these people, we will know that Jesus will help us too. As we read about the good things they did because of Jesus, we will want to love Jesus and be friends with Him just like the heroes of the Bible did.

Jesus said that the Bible tells us about Him (John 5:39). The Bible teaches that Jesus made us and that He's going to come and take us to live with Him. When we read the Bible, we are reading the words that He said, and we are seeing the things that He did. Do you want to know Jesus, the One who saves you? Then study the Bible.

Fill up your heart with words from the Bible. They will fill you up and make you happy. They are like water when you're thirsty and food when you are hungry (John 6:53, 63). Our bodies are made of the food we eat, and our hearts are made up of the things we think and talk about. If we want to be strong, beautiful Christians, we need to read Jesus' words in the Bible and keep them in our hearts.

Angels love to study about how God saves us. When we get to heaven and the new earth, we'll study about the way God saved us—and we'll sing about it too. So shouldn't we start paying attention now to how He saves us? Jesus gave so much for us. He loves us and was kind even when we didn't deserve it. We should think carefully about how good and sweet our dear Jesus is.

Jesus came to earth to save His people from sin. So let's think about Jesus and His love; then we'll believe more and be stronger than ever. Our prayers will be wiser. We will know that Jesus can take care of us—and that He will. We will get to know Him better every day.

As we spend time thinking about how good and perfect Jesus is, we will want to be changed. We will want to be just like Him.

He is holy and pure. Like we become hungry for food, we will become hungry to be like Him because we love Him so much. The more we think about Jesus, the more we will talk about Him and then everyone we meet will see Him in us.

Grow Your Mind!

Dad was working on some papers for work while Mom fixed supper. Christy played with Baby Daniel, and David sat at the kitchen table. He was working hard on his homework and sighed loudly. "I wish I were smarter!"

Dad looked up from his papers. "I know a way to become smarter."

"Really?" asked David. "How?"

"If you read the Bible, you'll become smarter."

"Really?"

Mom was standing by the sink, "If you finish your homework before supper, I'll read to everyone as soon as we've finished eating," she promised. "I think you'll like today's story."

Don't ever think that the Bible was written for only the very smartest people who study harder than anyone else. It was actually written for everyone. It explains the things we need to know to be saved in a way that we can understand. No one has to be lost or make mistakes unless they decide to do their own thing instead of what God wants them to.

A lot of people like to tell others their ideas about what the Bible teaches. Don't just listen to what someone tells you! Read or listen to the Bible *yourself.* If you let someone else think for you, you'll become lazy and forget how to think. Your mind is good and strong, but just like your muscles, if you don't exercise it, it will be weak.

Knowing God

Spend time thinking about good things—and, sometimes, about things that are kind of hard to understand. The exercise is good for you, and your mind will grow and be able to understand so much! Let the Bible be your teacher. If you find something in the Bible that you don't understand, just keep reading, because sooner or later you'll find something that will make it all clear, if you just pay attention.

Do you want your mind to be strong? Do you want to be able to understand things easily? The Bible is really good at growing your mind. If you study the Bible, it will give you better thoughts and understanding. If you want to be able to understand things, if you want to be good and pure, if you want to be strong in your choices, study the Bible. It will help you more than anything else can.

Don't hurry when you read or listen to the Bible because it won't do you much good if you do. If you don't pay attention, you can read every word in the whole Bible but never really learn the beautiful things it has to teach you. Choose a few verses or a story and think about what you are reading and pray about it until you truly understand it. That's better than reading a large amount—but never really learning what it is saying.

Take your Bible with you and read it or listen to it every time you get a chance. Memorize some verses too. Even when you are busy, you can be reading or thinking about the Bible. This will help it stick in your mind.

Do you want to be wise? Then pay careful attention to the Bible and pray often. Some things in the Bible are easy to understand, but some things are harder. You have to remember other things you have learned and think about how different parts of the Bible fit together. Think carefully about the things you learn from the Bible. As you do, you'll find many things there that are very special to you and helpful. As you pay attention to the words of the Bible and think about them, you'll find that you'll be happier and healthier every day.

Always pray before you study your Bible. Don't even open it until you pray, "Dear Father, please send Your Holy Spirit to help me understand the things You tell me in Your Word. Thank You. Amen."

The Bible tells us that when we try to understand what the Bible says and pray for Jesus to help us, that He sees and hears us and that angels will be with us.

The Holy Spirit shows us how wonderful Jesus is. It's His job to teach us about Jesus and His goodness. It's His job to teach us how to be saved. Jesus said that the Holy Spirit will teach us all about Him (John 16:14). Actually, the Holy Spirit is the only One who can really teach us about God.

God the Father gave Jesus to die so that people can be saved. His death proves that He loves us very much. And He has given the Holy Spirit to live in our hearts so that we can understand how much He loves us.

11 We Can Pray!

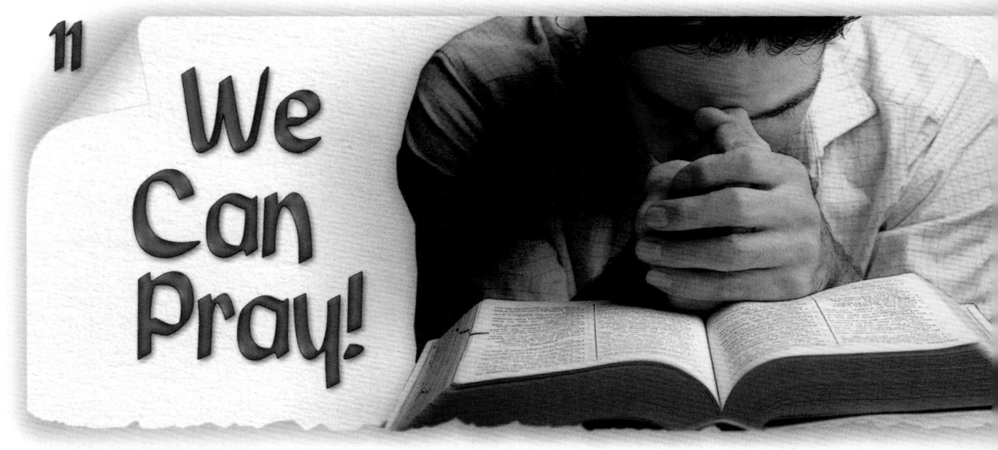

What's a Prayer?

David woke up earlier than usual and was looking out the window at the rain. He noticed that some worms had floated up on the sidewalk in the backyard and thought that was really cool. He ran into his parents' room to tell his dad what he had seen. Mr. Peppers was kneeling by an open window, and David thought he was looking out into the garden. "Hey, Dad," David said.

Mom motioned for David to be quiet. *"Shhh!"* she said. "Dad is praying. Don't bother him until he's finished."

David pulled away. "I need to tell Dad now before the worms crawl away!"

"No, David," Mom insisted. "This is Dad's special time with Jesus. Here's a new CD you can listen to for your own special time with Jesus. I think today's story will help you know what I mean."

God has all sorts of ways to talk to us. He speaks to us in the Bible and through the lovely things in the outside world.

He speaks to us by miracles and by feelings He puts in our hearts. But this is not enough. We need to talk to Him as well as listen to Him talk to us. We can share all our feelings with Him. If we want our hearts to be alive and strong, we need to share what we think and feel with our Friend, Jesus. We can think about Him—about the things He does and how kind He is. But even that is not really spending good time with Jesus. We need to tell Him about the things that happen in our lives.

Prayer is opening up our hearts to God and talking to Him the way we would to a friend. He doesn't need us to tell Him what we're like, but we need to talk to Him so that we can bring Him into our hearts more. Prayer doesn't bring God down to be with us, as some people think it does. When we pray, it's like our hearts go up to heaven to be with Him!

When Jesus was here on earth, He taught His disciples how to pray. He told them that if they ever needed anything, they should ask God. They shouldn't worry, but should give their worries to God. He promised them that God would hear them—and He will hear us too.

When Jesus lived on earth, He spent a lot of time praying. He understood the things that we need and how we aren't as strong as we should be. So He prayed for us.

He prayed all the time that God would make Him strong so that He would be all right when bad things happened to Him or when He had to do something hard. He is our Example. Jesus is our Brother and knows what it feels like to be tempted, just as we do. But He didn't have any sin in Him, so it hurt Him to see evil things. He often had hard times and a sad heart because sin was everywhere.

Because He was a person like us, Jesus knew He had to pray. And He was glad that He could pray! He felt better when He prayed; it really made Him happy to spend time with His Father. If our Savior, God's own Son, knew He needed to pray, just think how much more we need to pray! We are so weak and sinful. We need to pray hard and often.

Our Father in heaven wants to give us many good presents. His love is like a water fountain at which we can drink as much as we want anytime. So it's really amazing that we don't pray as often as we should. God is waiting. He wants to answer our prayers. He doesn't care if we're an important person or someone who's not very important at all. We shouldn't be shy to tell God what we want. The angels in heaven are surprised that the poor people on earth who are tempted all the time don't ask God for help. He wants to give them many things they need—but they don't even ask!

The angels love to be near God, and they bow when they are in His presence. They like spending time with Him more than anything else. It's amazing that the people on earth, who need so much help from God, often don't even know He's there. They seem perfectly happy to go their own way and not spend time with Him at all!

If you don't pray, Satan makes your heart dark. He whispers temptations in your ear, and if you haven't been praying, he can talk you into sinning. Prayer is a special appointment with God. Don't be shy about praying! Heaven is like a big room full of gifts and treasures, and prayer is like a key to open up that room.

If you forget to pray, you might become careless and find yourself doing bad things. Satan doesn't want you to be able to talk to God, so he does everything he can to keep you from praying. He wants to trap you and get you to sin.

Do you want God to listen to your prayers and answer them? First of all, you need to know how much you need Him. He gave us this promise, "I will pour water into the mouths of those who are thirsty, and I will send rain to the dry, cracked ground" (Isaiah

44:3). If you really want to be good—and you want it as much as you want food when you're hungry—then God will fill you up. But He can fill you with His goodness only if you are willing to let Him change you.

Do you know one of the reasons God likes to help us? Because we need His help so much. But we have to ask for His help. He says, "Ask for what you want, and I'll give it to you" (Matthew 7:7). When God sent Jesus to earth to die to save us, He was giving us the very best gift He could give. And He will give us everything else we could possibly need as well (Romans 8:32).

If you decide to hang on to sin—to keep doing bad things even when you know they're wrong—Jesus won't listen to you when you pray. But if you are sorry for your sins and want to be forgiven,

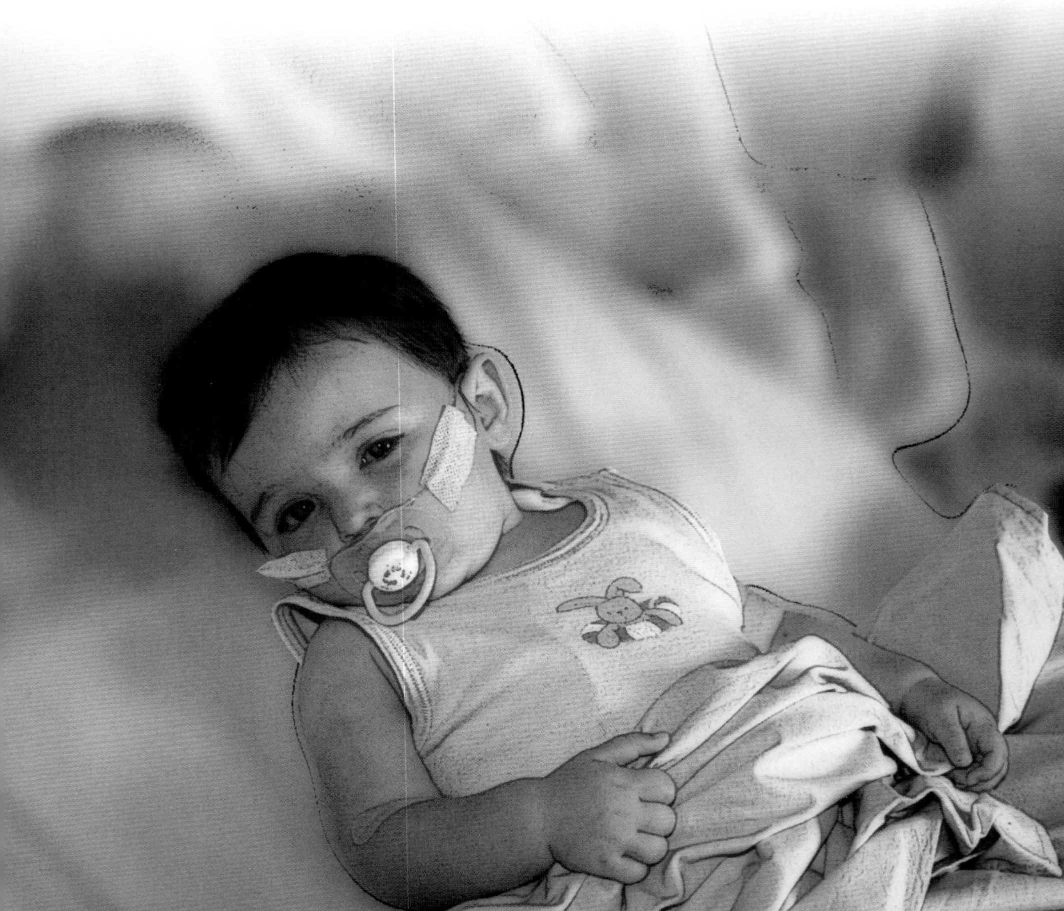

He will listen when you pray. When you make everything right the best way you know how, then you can know that God will hear your prayers.

God doesn't love you more when you do good things. He loves you because Jesus was so good and has promised to clean you up. But you still have work to do.

What If I Don't Get an Answer?

"Tell us a story, Mom!" David and Christy came running into the room.

Mom had just finished washing the dishes. She peeked in on Daniel, who was sleeping. "OK," she agreed. "Let me think. I know one.

"A long time ago, when you were a tiny baby, Christy, you got sick. You had a high fever, and you wouldn't eat or cry or anything. We were so worried about you!

"We prayed and prayed, but you didn't get better. We had to take you to the hospital.

"The doctor who took care of you had been a good Christian, but now he was discouraged and hadn't been going to church or praying for a long time. When he examined you, he thought you were going to die.

"He and his nurses worked so hard to make you well, but they didn't know what to do. We had known this doctor for some time, and we asked him to pray with us that you would get better. He agreed. We also prayed that Jesus would help him not be discouraged anymore.

"God worked a miracle, and you did get better, but not until a while later. You see, sometimes God uses our pain or sickness or sadness for a little while to reach someone else who needs to know about Him. If God doesn't answer our prayers at just the time we think He should, we can still trust Him because He knows what's best.

"When we finally left the hospital for the last time, the doctor knew Jesus better, and I think we did too. The doctor started going to church again, and he is a happy Christian now. Just think, Christy, he'll be in heaven now—maybe because of your illness!"

Christy was smiling, and David said, "Wow! I love that story!"

If you want your prayers to "get things done," you need to believe. God says that if you come to Him and look for Him, He will help you (Hebrews 11:6). Jesus told His special friends, the disciples, "When you pray, you may ask for whatever you need. If you believe, you will get what you asked for" (Mark 11:24). Do you really believe Him?

God's promises are very big, and He will do what He has promised. If you don't get exactly what you pray for at just the time you hoped you would, don't be upset! Keep on believing, because God does hear you, and He will answer.

Sometimes we don't know what's best for us, and we ask for something that wouldn't really make us happy. Our dear Father in heaven answers our prayers by giving us something *better.* If we could see how everything will work out in the end, we'd see that God gives us what we would really want if we understood the whole story.

If it seems that God hasn't answered your prayers, remember that He has promised to hear you. You'll get your answer at just the right time. God will give you what you need the most. But don't think that God will answer your prayers in exactly the way you ask Him to. He's too smart to make a mistake, and He's so good that He'll always give you the very best when you choose to obey. Don't be afraid to believe in God, even if He doesn't give the answer you want right away. Remember, He has promised, "Ask, and I will give you what you need."

If you decide not to believe God's promises until you can figure everything out and understand it, you'll be stressed and worried. Don't think about all the things you are afraid of. When you come to God just the way you are, knowing that you can't do everything by yourself, He can help you. He will listen to you, and His light will shine into your hearts and make you feel better.

Do you want to learn to be friends with God? Do you want to understand what He is like? You can do this by praying with all your heart. You may not feel that Jesus is near, but He is close to you, and He is ready to show you His love. You may not be able to feel His warm hugs, but you need to remember that He is there just the same, covering you up in His love.

If you want to receive the gifts that you ask God for, you must keep praying, because that's how it works. Do you want to grow and be a better Christian? Keep praying! Be ready to pray all the time. Keep on praying and giving thanks because Jesus is listening (Romans 12:12; Colossians 4:2).

The disciple Peter tells us to "be serious and pay attention to your prayers" (1 Peter 4:7). And the apostle Paul says, "Tell God just what you need and be thankful at the same time" (Philippians 4:6). We should pray to God. This is how we stay close to Jesus and learn to live in His love (Jude 20, 21). If we want to be best friends with God, we need to pray and pray and pray. God will fill up our lives, and then we will be able to share His love and goodness.

Places to Pray

"But I don't want to go to prayer meeting!" complained David. "I don't like to sit for that long!"

Dad frowned. "But you like to go to church."

"That's different. Why should I go to prayer meeting?"

"Do you love Jesus?" asked Dad. "You said you want to know Him better."

"Well I do, but—"

"There are lots of places to pray, but it's really good for you to go and listen and pray with other people too. It'll help you grow if you pay attention. Why don't you listen to today's selection on the CD before we go? Maybe it'll help."

It's important that you pray often. Don't let anything get in your way. Do all you can to stay friends with Jesus. If you know of a place where people are getting together to pray, make sure you go every time. If you're really trying to know God better, you will go to every prayer meeting you can; good things come from praying together with other people. You'll learn more about heaven and God's love.

Pray with your family too. But, most important, remember to pray by yourself, because this is what will make you a strong Christian. You can't be a real Christian if you don't pray. It's not enough to pray with your family, and it's not enough to pray at church. When you are all by yourself, you should tell God everything that is on your mind. These prayers are no one else's business. They are between you and God only. Find a quiet time and a quiet place to pray to God alone.

You don't have to get excited when you pray; just talk to God like you would to a friend. He will hear your prayers and give you a sweet, happy heart. If you spend time with God and believe His promises, your heart will be filled with His love and made strong against Satan.

If you pray early in the day in your special place, you will be able to talk to God all day long too. That's how Enoch in the Bible stayed so close to God. God loves to hear the quiet prayers that we whisper from our hearts as we work and play. If we keep God in our hearts like this, Satan cannot win over us.

You can pray to God anytime or anywhere. Nothing can stop you. If you are in a crowded, busy place, or if you are doing your chores, you can ask God to help you and teach you. You may have your quiet prayer time with God wherever you are. You should keep giving your heart to Jesus all day long, every day. Keep asking Him to come into your heart and fill you with good things.

Even when there are bad things going on around you, you don't have to be a part of it. You can carry heaven around in your heart. You don't have to choose bad thoughts. You can lift your heart up to God by praying. If you want God to be with you, just let Him keep coming in. You can be good and carry goodness around in your heart all the time. You can learn to be His very dear friend.

Like Jesus Prayed

David had been reading a book he had borrowed from a friend. He looked up at his mother, who was folding baby clothes.

"If you could have one wish, Mom, what would it be?"

"Oh that's easy. I would want to be more like Jesus."

"Really? Do you think that wish will come true?"

"Yes, I know it will if I do what Jesus did."

David wasn't sure what she meant. "What do you mean, Mom?"

"Well, if I learn to pray like Jesus prayed, if I learn to spend time with our Father in heaven like He did, I will become more like Him."

"Really? I think I wish that too."

"Why don't you go get your sister and the book? I think I hear little Daniel awake. I'll be back in a minute."

We need to understand Jesus better than we do. We need to understand heaven. We must be kind and good and holy, and if we want this to happen, we should ask God to teach us all about heaven.

Let God help you see what heaven is like. If you stay close to God, then when something bad comes along, you will automatically think about Him. You can go to God whenever you need Him.

We Can Pray!

Tell God about everything in your life. Tell Him what you want and what makes you happy. Tell Him what makes you sad and what you worry about. Tell Him what scares you too. You can't bother Him or make Him tired. He knows you so well, that He even knows how many hairs you have on your head. He really loves you and pays attention to what you care about. "The Lord is full of kindness and mercy" (James 5:11). His heart is full of love, and He understands when you are sad. If something is bothering you, tell God. Nothing is too hard for Him to handle! He is big enough to hold the planets up and to take care of everything all at once. If something bothers your heart, then it's important enough for God to pay attention to it and help you. No matter how bad you have been, He understands; your worst troubles are easy for Him to take care of. Our dear Father sees every bad thing that happens to you. He also watches when you're worried or when you're happy. He hears you every time you pray to Him. God is really good at "healing broken hearts and soothing their pain" (Psalm 147:3). He loves you so much that it's like you are the very best friend He has ever had. He takes care of you as if you were His only precious child.

Jesus says that when we ask for anything in His name, God will hear us because He loves us. Jesus has chosen us as His special children, and He will ask His Father to give us what we ask for (John 16:26, 27; 15:16). But just saying, "Dear Jesus," at the beginning of your prayer, or saying, "In Jesus' name, Amen," at the close of your prayer isn't really praying in Jesus' name. Praying in Jesus' name means to pray like Jesus prayed. We ask for what *He* wants, and we believe His promises. Then we can trust Him, and we can do the things He wants us to do. That's how we really pray in Jesus' name.

Some people go off by themselves away from other people so they can spend all their time alone, worshiping and praying.

That's not what Jesus wants us to do! He wants us to live like He did. Jesus did spend some of His time off by Himself praying. But then He would spend time with people—helping them and teaching them. If all you ever do is pray, soon you won't pray anymore, or your prayers will become boring and empty. If you stop spending time visiting with people and helping them, if you stop working like Jesus worked, pretty soon you'll not have anything else to pray about. Your prayers will become

selfish because you won't know what other people need anymore. You should pray that you will be strong to do the work Jesus assigns you.

Happy in Jesus

"No Christy, we're not going to the park this afternoon. I have a lot to do before tomorrow, and we don't have time." When Mrs. Peppers turned around to see if Christy understood, she burst out laughing. "You look awful! Don't you know that Christians aren't supposed to have donkey faces?"

David and Christy looked at each other, and Christy squinted her eyes.

"What does that mean?" they asked together.

Mom put her face up close to Christy's. "It means your face looks looooong and sad, and Christians are supposed to be happy. OK, I think it's story time."

We need to spend time encouraging other Christians, helping each other be strong and work for God. If we don't do this, soon the Bible won't seem so real or important to us anymore. We'll stop knowing how to live as Christians should live. We should be kind and loving to other Christians. We should share and help others—or we aren't doing the work that Jesus wants us to do. If we learn to be friendly and get along with people, we can be a better help to God.

Do you want a happier heart? Then you should spend time with other Christians and talk about God's love and how He saves us. If you learn more about our Father in heaven every day, then you'll want to tell people about His love. If you tell other people about God's love, you'll feel happy and encouraged. Do you want

Jesus to be very close to you? Then you must think about Him and talk about Him.

How many times today has God given you little gifts of love? Every time you see something that God has made for you or shared with you, you should think about Him and His goodness. This will help you enjoy talking and singing about Him.

Here on earth we talk about all sorts of interesting things that we see and hear. We talk to our friends because we love them. It's the same with God. We should think about Him and talk with Him because we love Him. We need to talk about how good and strong He is. God gives us many lovely things so we can remember Him and think about Him. Stop thinking about all the little unimportant things around you. Look up and think about Jesus, who will save you if you come to Him (Hebrews 7:25).

We need to spend a lot more time praising God, because He is so good and gives us so many good things (Psalm 107:8). We shouldn't spend time with Him just so we can pray and ask for things. We should tell Him "thank You" for the wonderful gifts He has given us. We don't say "thank You" nearly as often as we should.

A long time ago, when God's people, the Israelites, went to church, God told them to be happy and joyful in everything that they did (Deuteronomy 12:7). He said that they should sing happy songs and have cheerful hearts. God doesn't like sadness and gloominess.

Our God is a kind Father with a soft heart. Don't think that working for Him makes you sad or stressed out. Worshiping Jesus and working for Him should make you happy. God has given us a wonderful gift by saving us, and He doesn't want us to act sad and tired like slaves. He is your best Friend, and when you worship Him, He wants to be with you. He will make you happy and comfort you when you're upset. He'll fill your heart with joy and love and make you glad.

We Can Pray!

God wants you to have fun and be happy while you do the things He asks you to do. When you worship Him, you will learn all sorts of nice things to help you be happier when you work and play and study. He will make you strong to always tell the truth and to be faithful and work hard.

Think about how Jesus died for you, because this is how He saves you. You should think about this and talk about this. It should make you really happy. Always think about the wonderful things that God has given to you. When you understand how much He loves you, you will be willing to trust Him in everything and to obey Him.

By praising God and learning to be thankful, we will understand what heaven is like. In heaven, the angels sing and play beautiful music to praise God. We, too, should be thankful and sing to Him with all our hearts (Isaiah 51:3).

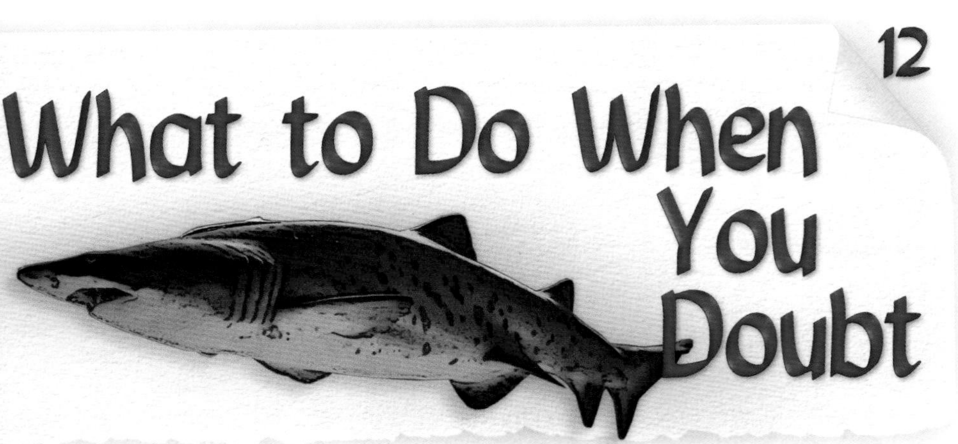

12 What to Do When You Doubt

It's Up to You

David and Christy were watching a science video about sharks. The man on the video said that sharks came from earlier kinds of fish and slowly changed over millions and millions of years into what they are today.

"How can people believe that stuff?" asked David. "God made the sharks."

"You know, David," Mom replied, "sometimes people find something that they don't like about God. They become upset, and the more they think about it, the more they wonder if there is a God at all. Finally they decide they just can't believe in Him anymore."

David looked serious. "Sometimes I've wondered about God too. I mean, I've never seen Him."

Mom smiled. "Oh, everyone has wondered about God before. But what matters is what you do about your questions."

"What *should* you do about them?" David wanted to know.

"All right," Mom said. "Come sit down. Let's read today's story."

What to Do When You Doubt

Sometimes people have a hard time believing in God. This is called *doubt*. New Christians, especially, have trouble with doubt. There are lots of things in the Bible that you just can't understand, so Satan wants you to believe that none of it is true. Do you want to get rid of doubt? Do you want to be able to believe with all your heart?

God gives us lots of things to help us believe. God is real, and He's really good. Everything He says in the Bible is true, and we have good reasons to believe it. But we can still doubt if we want to. We don't have to believe. We can believe because we have good reasons to believe, but God doesn't prove everything. There will always be some things that are hard to understand and reasons not to believe them—if you don't want to. But if you want to believe, you can always find plenty of reasons to do so, and God will help you believe.

Your mind is too small and not smart enough to understand God completely. He is so big and wonderful that even the smartest, most educated person in the whole world can't understand everything about God! Job, in the Bible, says, "Do you think you can understand God by trying really hard? Can you get to know God perfectly? He's as high as heaven, so what do you think you can do? Understanding Him is so deep that we can never expect to know everything about Him" (Job 11:7, 8).

Paul, the apostle, says, "Knowing God and His wisdom is so deep! He judges fairly when we wouldn't even understand what to do! We could never understand the way that God works" (Romans 11:33). But even though there are some things about

God that we can't understand, we can know that He is holy and fair (Psalm 97:2). We certainly can understand enough about God and the way He treats us to see that He loves us and is kind.

We can also see that He is very strong. How much can we understand about God? We can understand just enough to help us. He lets us understand what's best for us to understand. For anything more than that, we can trust Him because He is strong and He loves us.

Ever since people started disobeying God, there have been some things too hard for us to understand. We can't ever totally understand how Jesus became a person or how He woke up from being dead. We can never really understand how God is able to give someone a brand-new heart. There are a lot of things in the Bible that we can't completely understand. But that's no reason to not believe in God! After all, there are lots of things in life that we can't understand.

Little bugs and germs and other kinds of life are very simple to God, but the smartest men in the world can't figure out everything about them. There are things everywhere in nature that we can't understand, so we shouldn't be surprised that there are things about God that we don't understand. The problem is that sometimes people don't *want* to believe. In the Bible, God has given us plenty of good reasons to believe in Him, so we must not doubt just because we can't understand.

Peter, the disciple, says, "There are things in the Bible that are hard to understand. People who don't know much or who only try to be Christians sometimes get strange ideas from these things and end up not making it to heaven" (2 Peter 3:16). Some people point to these things in the Bible that are hard to understand and say that this is a good reason not to believe in the Bible at all. But actually, these puzzles can help us believe that the Bible is God's Book! If all the things the Bible says about

God were easy to understand and if we know everything there is to know about God, then how would God be any different from us? The Bible shows us how big and strong and awesome God really is. It shows us that He is the kind of God we can believe in!

The Bible teaches us true things and makes it easy for us to understand many things. God knew just what to say in the Bible so that we could learn the very things we need to know when we read it. The Bible is exciting and interesting enough for the smartest people, but it is simple enough that it can teach anyone how to be saved.

The things that the Bible teaches us about how to be saved are so big and great and wonderful that we can never understand them completely. So we have to believe that everything it says is true—because God said so. In the Bible, God tells us how to believe in Jesus and be saved. He has a plan to save us, and we can know what we need to do. But there are things about God's plan that we don't fully understand, so we study more and try to know God better every day. God likes it when we try to get to know Him better. The more we try to figure out the Bible, the more we will know that it is God's Book—and the more we will see how great the Bible is.

God's Still Bigger

"Remember what we talked about yesterday?" Mom asked, as she sat at the foot of Christy's bed.

"About God?" asked David.

"Yes. In some ways, I think it's good that we don't understand everything in the Bible."

"Why?" David wanted to know.

"Because that means we're smart." Mom watched the children. They weren't sure what Mom meant.

"It means," their mother continued, "you are smart enough to know that you are not as smart as God. You need to remember that God is bigger and smarter than you are."

She opened up the book and started to read.

If you admit that you can't understand everything in the Bible, you're just saying that you are not as big as God is.

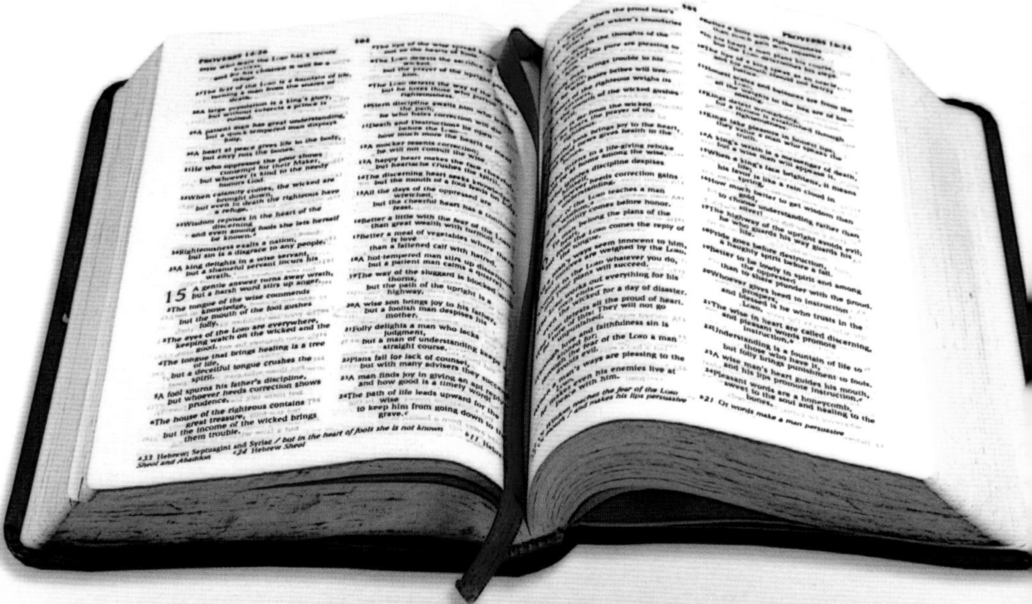

People who don't love God and who want to doubt choose not to pay attention to anything the Bible says. They want to do away with it. Even some people who say they believe the Bible have the same problem. If you choose not to believe, you will turn away from God (Hebrews 3:12). You should carefully study the things in the Bible that are hard to understand. You should be curious and look for God's answers (1 Corinthians 2:10). There are some things we'll never understand, but some things only *seem* to be too hard to understand. If we study, God will teach us those things (Deuteronomy 29:29).

Satan likes to make us lazy. He doesn't like curious people. Some people feel bad if they can't understand every verse in the Bible. They're embarrassed to admit they don't understand the Bible! They don't want to wait for God to teach them. They think that their minds should be good enough to understand whatever they want to understand, and when they can't, they throw out the whole Bible and say that it's a bunch of lies.

Sometimes people say that the Bible teaches something that it really doesn't teach at all. It may be something that someone just made up. It may be something that goes against everything that the Bible really teaches. This can confuse people and make them doubt God.

If we could understand God completely, then we wouldn't have anymore growing to do. We wouldn't have anything else to learn, and our hearts wouldn't have any room to grow. Then God wouldn't be smarter than we are.

We should be so thankful that that's not the way it works! God is bigger than anything else—and then still bigger than that! He has many, many things to teach us (Colossians 2:3). For ever and ever, we can still search and learn and grow—and still understand only a little bit of how smart and good and strong our God really is!

Even now God wants us always to be learning more about Him and growing. God will light up our minds by His Holy Spirit; this is the only way we can learn more about the Bible. We can understand truth about God only when the Holy Spirit helps us. He will teach us the deepest secrets about God (1 Corinthians 2:11, 10). Jesus said, "When the Holy Spirit comes into your heart, He will teach you everything that is true. He will show you everything about Me" (John 16:13, 14).

Stretch Your Brain

"You're it!" squealed Christy, slapping David on the back.

"I quit!" said David, who was breathing fast. "What are you doing, Mom?" David looked over his mother's shoulder.

"I'm making a puzzle out of a Bible verse. See?" She held it up.

"I thought you said that it's foolish to waste a bunch of time on games."

"Yes, but this isn't just some silly game. This is special. God wants us to use our brains and to learn as much as we can."

(You can see the game Mom made on page 127. You can even play it, if you want to!)

After David spent some time with Mom's puzzle, he asked if she would read the next part of the book. So Mom picked up the book, and the children gathered around her.

God wants you to think. When you study the Bible, it lifts your mind and teaches you to think like nothing else can. But be careful not to think yourself too smart, because you can still become confused or not understand something that you should. It is easier, sometimes, for little children to believe and trust God than it is for grown-ups. But everyone must be willing to learn and listen to the Holy Spirit if they want to understand the Bible. Be ready to learn and ask the Holy Spirit to teach you.

You need to know that you need God. You're never so good that you can do without Him. If you remember how strong and smart He is, you will never forget this. When you study the Bible, you should come before God quietly and lovingly. Remember that God is bigger than you are and that you need to obey

Him. Love and worship Him with all your heart and remember that He is the God who has been around forever and will never go away.

Many things may seem hard to understand at first, but God will help you understand if you just ask Him and try to understand. But if you don't let God's Holy Spirit help you, you'll always get mixed up! Sometimes you can read the Bible or listen to it and just end up confused. When you don't treat the Bible reverently and you don't pray to God for help—or when you don't think about God and obey what you understand—you'll get confused and sad and will have a hard time believing at all. Then you'll end up being more confused than ever, and Satan can take over your thoughts and give you all sorts of strange ideas about the Bible.

Even if people are really smart, they're probably going to make mistakes in understanding the Bible if they don't really *want* to know what God wants them to do. Don't listen to what someone like this may tell you. If people are just looking for reasons to believe that the Bible isn't important, they won't be able to understand much at all. They'll find all sorts of things to make the Bible hard to understand, and even the simple, easy things will become confusing to them.

Do you want to know why most people doubt and have trouble believing the Bible? Usually, it's because that person loves to sin. The Bible is God's Word, and it tells us things that we must do or must stop doing. If someone loves to sin and disobey, he or she doesn't want to believe that the Bible is true.

If you want to really know what is true and right, you have to want to know it enough to obey it. If you decide, "When I find out what God wants, I will obey," then you'll find lots of reasons to believe the Bible. If you choose to obey, then you will begin to understand many things that you need to know to be saved.

Do You Want to Understand?

Mr. Dean and Mr. Peppers had been good friends for a while. Mr. Peppers had helped Mr. Dean meet Jesus. This evening, he had eaten supper with the Peppers family because his wife, Sue, was out of town for a few days.

"I've been arguing with Sue," Mr. Dean told them as he pushed away from the table. "She says she can't understand the Bible. I told her that if she would just obey what she already knows, then God will show her how to understand other things. But she won't listen! I tell her almost every day."

When Mr. Dean said that, David noticed Mom smile as she began clearing the table. Later, he asked her, "Why were you smiling? What was funny?"

"Oh, it wasn't really funny," Mom answered. "I smiled because Mr. Dean gets so excited. He's a new Christian, and he shouldn't argue with his wife." Then Mom looked serious. "But Mr. Dean *is* right," she added.

"You mean I can help myself understand the Bible?" David asked.

"Yes, in a way. If you pray and then obey, God will teach you more."

Jesus said, "If a person wants to do what God asks, He will be able to understand the things that he needs to understand" (John 7:17). Instead of asking and fussing and worrying about all the things in the Bible that you don't understand, pay attention to what you already know. If you do this, you'll learn more. With God's love and power making you strong, you should do everything you know you're supposed to do. Then you will start to understand the things that you haven't been able to understand before.

What to Do When You Doubt

Everyone can look at the things that have happened in their own lives. That is something that everyone has that is a good reason for believing. Do you want to know if God is telling the truth? You can prove it. Learn to know Him (Psalm 34:8). Obey Him and start counting on Him to make you strong. He'll give you a new heart if you ask Him for one. Don't just believe what someone else tells you. God always keeps His promises—He always will. When you let God stay close to you, all of your doubt and sadness will go away.

Paul, Jesus' special friend, says that "God has made us free from darkness and has made us His children" (Colossians 1:13). Everyone who gets a new heart and a new life can know that God is true (John 3:33). That person can tell everyone that Jesus helped him or her when he or she needed it—that Jesus gave him or her everything he or she needed.

That person can say, "The Bible shows me Jesus. I believe in Jesus because He is God and He has saved me. I believe in the Bible because that's how God talks to me." You can know in your own heart that the Bible is real and true and that Jesus is God's Son. We know that this is not a lie!

In the Bible, Peter tells us to "keep growing in Jesus' love and power. Keep learning more about Him because He saved us" (2 Peter 3:18). When God's people grow the way they're supposed to, they'll understand the Bible more and more. They will learn new and beautiful things. This is how it has been with Christians for as long as there have been Christians, and it will always be this way. "The road that the good man walks on will get clearer and easier to see as he goes on, just like walking in the morning when the sun is coming up" (Proverbs 4:18).

You can trust God to make you smarter and to make your heart more like His. You can become better and better friends with Him. You can be happy because, even though sometimes you have been confused or upset by things that have happened to you, God will explain everything someday. Even though you had a hard time understanding things before, God will show you how everything will work out beautifully in the end. "Right now we understand only a few things, but someday soon we'll understand many things. I know only part of what I need to know right now, but soon I will know everything I need to know" (1 Corinthians 13:12).

Bible Word Puzzle

How many of the following hidden words can you find in this puzzle? They are all from Proverbs 4:18, 19; John 16:13, 14; and 1 Corinthians 13:12 in the New King James Version. (Remember words can run up, down, across, or diagonally!)

path	face	wicked
stumble	perfect	sun
shining	mirror	just
brighter	darkness	spirit
glorify	tell	truth
declare	guide	speak
hears	things	mine

B W E U Q L O M I R R O R C A M E A S V

R L G P V L D F L A S E D R M D I A H K

H U P S O F S J U S T A B E O H I N L G

J E E I G O B A L H E A R S C T S P E R

Q M R P N S W E G U I D E J V L G K N Z

A T F G I O L I A J F Z A U I O A L O U

S P E A K W R T C I A V C T O Y J R D R

L R C R A B G R D K C T E H L F X M E H

T H T L R N E U O R E P J I S I O O S B

I B W D I P A T H R H D T N U R E T K W

R E O N C D N H E S A E U G R O J G R T

I B I G E S V D A R K N E S S L M Q U E

P H L W N U S T R N U F K N T G P R A S

S G H I L M T V Y S T E L L P A J P B R

S T U M B L E E N O P G R S C L A R D J

13 Being Happy in Jesus

Satan's Lies and a Letter From God

After supper, Dad was sitting on the couch. He held Daniel in one arm and a picture album in his other hand. David and Christy sat on each side of Dad as they looked at pictures of Grandma and Grandpa.

"I like pictures," David said after a while. "But just pictures aren't enough. I wish Grandma and Grandpa were here!"

"Me, too," agreed Dad. "But a picture is better than nothing. Hey, do you know you are a picture?"

Christy giggled.

"What do you mean?" asked David.

"Well, we're supposed to show people what Jesus is like—kind of like a picture helps us remember what Grandma and Grandpa are like. So we're a picture to other people."

Do you know what your job is? Your job is to show people what Jesus is like. By being good and kind, you can show others that Jesus is good and kind. Jesus showed us what His Father was like, and we must show the whole world that Jesus has a soft heart and loves each person. The Father sent Jesus to do this job, and so now Jesus sends us to do the same thing. God was in Jesus, shining out. And Jesus wants to be in your heart to shine out to other people too (John 17:18, 23).

The Bible says that we're supposed to be like a love letter that Jesus wrote to the world, telling them how much He loves them (2 Corinthians 3:3, 2). If you are Jesus' child, then you are like a letter to your family and your neighborhood and your city, telling them what Jesus wants them to know. Jesus is living in your heart, and He wants to talk to people who don't know Him yet.

Some people don't read the Bible, or they don't understand what they read. Maybe they don't understand that all the beautiful things in the world are God's presents to them. But if you really belong to Jesus, maybe you're the one who can teach them about His goodness and love, and then maybe they will want to work for Jesus too!

This world is like a dark place because not many people know Jesus. Christians are like a flashlight to light the way and show other people how to get to heaven. Jesus is the light that shines out of them. When other people see what a Christian does and how a Christian acts, they should learn about Jesus.

If you show other people what Jesus is like, they will see that it is fun to work for Him—because it is! Christians who complain and act gloomy and sad are lying about God. That is not what it means to be a Christian. They act as if God doesn't want His children to be happy, and so they are really telling lies about God.

Satan loves it when he can make God's children sad and doubt. He is pleased when we don't trust God or don't think He's strong enough to take care of us. Satan wants us to think that God's way will make us miserable and unhappy. Satan teaches people that God doesn't feel sorry when we're sad and that He doesn't really love us. Satan lies about God whenever he can, and he fills people's heads with false ideas about God.

Sometimes we think about the lies that Satan tells and wonder whether God really doesn't love us very much. Then we start complaining and grumbling about God. Satan wants to make Christians sad. He wants us to think that being a Christian is hard and too much work. If a Christian acts as if that is true, he's helping Satan tell his lies.

Collecting Flowers and Blessings

Mrs. Peppers was cutting vegetables for lunch when David sat on the floor beside her. He frowned and sighed.

"What's wrong?" Mom asked.

"The cat scratched me. My stomach hurts. Christy's asleep. And I'm bored. I just feel grumpy!"

"Well, I'm almost finished making lunch," Mom replied. "If you will go get the book, I'll read to you—just you and me. Does that sound good?"

David ran into the next room to get the book. And soon he and Mom were sitting down by a bright window to read.

Many people spend a lot of time thinking about all the bad things they've done and the mistakes they've made. They think about the sad things in their lives, and all this fills them with sadness. Some people are like two ladies in a dream. In the dream, the ladies were walking through a garden, being showed around by the gardener. One lady was picking flowers and smelling their lovely perfume. But the other lady, who was beside her, said, "Look at those ugly thorns! They are in my way." She started crying because she couldn't get through the thorns.

But the whole time, she wasn't walking on the path. She was walking where all the thorns and prickles were! She sadly said, "Isn't it awful that this beautiful garden is all filled with thorns?" But the gardener said, "Leave the thorns alone, because they'll just hurt you. Instead, pick the roses and lilies and other flowers."

Have you had good, happy times in your life? Have you had times when you were so happy with God that you thought your heart was full? Have good things happened to you? God's promises are all around you, kind of like the flowers in the garden in the dream. Let the sweet beauty of God's promises fill your heart and make you happy!

The thorns and prickles will just hurt you. If you collect all the bad things and share them with others, you are ignoring God's goodness. And you are also making life harder for other people.

It's not very smart to keep thinking about the bad things in your life. Don't sit around remembering your sad times and your sins. Stop talking about them and fussing about them until your heart breaks! When you are sad, your heart is filled with darkness. It makes it harder to see God's light, and you make others around you sad.

Thank God for the good times He's given you. Think about all the things that make you happy—your blessings. Maybe even make a list of all your blessings so you can think about them all the time. Here are some of the good things in your life: Jesus came from heaven to be a human and save us from Satan. Jesus won the war over Satan, so now we can go to heaven. We don't have to be stuck sinning anymore, because we are friends with God again. Now we can believe in Jesus and be holy and good; and we can go to be with Him at His throne. All these are things that God likes you to think about.

When we doubt God's love and don't believe His promises, we dishonor God, and we make Him sad. How would your mom feel

if you always complained about her and thought she was mean? How would she feel if you told her, "You always try to make my whole life miserable and sad! You don't really love me"? It would break her heart and make her so sad, wouldn't it?

God doesn't like you to act that way about Him either. He gave His only Son to die for you just so that you could live. And you can be sure that He will give you everything that is best for you to have (Romans 8:32). But sometimes people act as if God doesn't really love them at all. They think, *Well, maybe God loves other people, but He doesn't love me.*

All this just hurts your own heart. Every time you say something about not believing God, you're letting Satan tempt you more. It makes you think about doubt more, and sometimes it even chases the angels away! When Satan tries to talk you into thinking sad thoughts or not believing God, don't say a word about not believing. When you feel sad or think you can't believe in God, don't talk about it. Don't even think about it, because if you let Satan trick you into thinking that way, it will make you doubt even more. It can also make other people sad and discouraged, and you might not ever be able to help them be happy and strong again. Maybe you can get over your sad feelings, but you don't know if these other people will be able to. So don't talk about your doubts or fears! It's very important to talk only about things that help other people to believe and be strong.

Angels are listening to what you say about Jesus. Talk about your wonderful Jesus and how He is working to help you. When you are with your friends, talk about God and how good He is. This will help them think good things about Jesus too.

Don't Talk About the Bad Things!

The next morning David peeked around the corner. Mom was changing Daniel's diaper.

"Mom, do you think my cat scratch is infected? It hurts more today. Are we going to do anything fun today? I'm not feeling very well—"

"Stop!" Mom laughed. "Do you remember our story about collecting flowers?"

David grinned in spite of himself. "Yes, but I'm still thinking about my cat scratch. I need to tell someone about it! What do you want me to do?"

"Go get your sister. I think we need another story."

Mom fastened Baby Daniel's clothes and sat down in her favorite chair.

Everyone has bad things that happen to them. It's hard to deal with sad times, and it's hard to say No when Satan tempts us. But don't tell all these things to other people. Pray to God and tell it all to Him. When you're having a hard time believing or when you're discouraged, make it your rule to never, ever talk about it. If you talk instead about trust and happiness, you can really be a big help to other people. You can help make them strong.

A lot of people have hard temptations and feel tired and sad. Some of these people might be almost ready to give up. Don't make them sad! Help them be happy by speaking good, happy words to them. Jesus' light can shine out of you. Remember, you're not all by yourself—there are other people to help along the way (Roman 14:7). You can be a help to someone, or you can discourage someone and make them not want Jesus—just by the words you say.

Some people don't understand what Jesus was like when He was here on earth. They think that He wasn't very friendly or happy. They think He was hard and strict and kind of sad.

Being Happy in Jesus

Some people are sad Christians because they think that is how Jesus is.

Some people like to say that Jesus cried, but no one ever saw Him smile. It's true that Jesus had a lot of sadness in His life, because He opened up His heart to people and felt all their sadness and hurting. But even though He gave and gave to others, and even though He sometimes hurt and had serious things to think about, He didn't have a sad, broken heart. He didn't walk around looking sad. He had a peaceful, quiet, happy look on His face. His heart was full of joy, and He shared rest and peace and happiness with everyone around Him.

Jesus was very serious and very careful about everything He did. But He was never gloomy or depressed. Christians should be serious and know that they have important things to do. They won't be silly, and they won't be rude, smart alecks. But that doesn't stop them from being cheerful. A Christian will have bright, smiling face. Jesus didn't come so that everyone could help Him and work for Him. He came to be a helper. When you love people like Jesus did, you will be a happy helper too.

If spend your time thinking about the mean things that people have done to you, you won't be able to love those people like Jesus does. If you think about Jesus and how much He loves you, then you'll be able to love others in the same way. We should love each other and be respectful, even when other people don't treat us very well.

Don't trust yourself. Remember that you are nothing without Jesus. Learn to be patient when other people aren't perfect. If you do that, you won't be selfish anymore. You'll have a big heart and want to share with others.

King David said, "If you trust God and do good things to other people, you will have a long life, and you will have all the food you need" (Psalm 37:3). Bad things will happen to you every day. And it's easy to talk to other people about the bad things that have happened to you. Sometimes we talk about bad things that haven't even happened yet, but that we are afraid *might* happen! We talk about how worried we are. People listening to us might think we didn't have Jesus to take care of us! He is waiting to hear what we have to say, and He is ready to help us.

Some people are always afraid, always worrying about things. Every day they can see God's many presents all around them, and they use the many things that He has given them. But they don't even notice all the good things that God has given them right now. They just keep thinking about some bad thing—either something that has actually happened to them or something that might happen. We can make little, tiny problems look so big that we can't see all the good things or remember to say thank You for God's blessings. Hard times should make us go to God for help, but, instead, we let them pull us away from God because we like to complain.

Is it good for us to doubt like this? Shouldn't we trust God? Yes, we should be thankful! Jesus is our Friend, and all the angels want to make us happy. Don't let the problems and troubles in life make you upset. If you do, you'll always have something to worry about. Don't have a bad attitude that just upsets you and makes you tired, because it doesn't help you at all.

Little Worries and a Sermon on a Mountain

David brought the book to Mom. She was reading a letter. "When are you going to finish your letter?" he asked. "I want a story. What is the story about today?"

"You know Dad is preaching the sermon tomorrow in church, don't you?"

"Yes," replied David. "I saw him studying this afternoon. Why?"

"Because today's story is about a sermon. It is about the best sermon ever," Mom said.

"Wow! Who preached that sermon?"

"We'll see," said Mom. "Christy, bring Daniel in here. Let's have a story!"

You may be confused about something you need to figure out. It may look like you have no hope and that you're going to lose everything. Don't be discouraged and sad! Give your sadness to

Jesus and stay calm and happy. Pray that God will help you do the best you can. Then do the very best job you know how. Jesus has promised to help us, but only if we're trying too. When you trust in Jesus and do all you can, then just take whatever happens and keep a happy heart.

God doesn't want you to be sad and burdened with worries. But He's honest too. He doesn't try to tell us that nothing bad will ever happen to us. He knows that bad things will come. He doesn't promise to keep every bad thing away from us, but He does promise to help us meet them and get through them. Jesus tells us that we will have problems, but not to worry, because He is in charge of everything (John 17:15; 16:33).

One day, Jesus preached a very famous sermon up on a mountainside. In His sermon, He taught important lessons about trusting God. You can learn a lot if you pay attention to what Jesus said. He pointed to the birds that were singing nearby. They praised God with their songs and didn't worry at all. They didn't have to work hard planting gardens and waiting for food to grow. "Yet," Jesus said, "God takes care of them." Then He added, "You are so much more important than the little birds!" (Matthew 6:26).

God gives everyone what they need, and His hand is open with plenty of gifts. The birds are so little, but they aren't too little for God to notice and care for. We're more important than the birds (Matthew 6:26). Of course, God doesn't drop food right into the birds' mouths, but He does make food grow for them to eat. They have to collect the little seeds that God gives them, and they have to build nests for their babies. The whole time they are working, they are singing because God has given them what they need. You are smart, and you can know and love God; you're worth a lot more than the birds. Don't you think God will give you what you need if you just trust Him?

Being Happy in Jesus

Then Jesus pointed to the flowers growing all around Him. They were bright and beautiful because God made them that way. Jesus said, "Think about the lilies and how they grow." These little flowers are more beautiful than the richest king in his fanciest clothes. Then Jesus said, "If God dresses the grass so nicely with all the flowers, don't you think He'll give you clothes? You just don't believe enough!" (Matthew 6:28). God is the greatest artist, and He takes time to paint each little flower in lovely colors even though they don't last very long. You are made to be like God, so think how much more He will pay attention to you! Jesus was teaching a very important lesson to those who worry and doubt.

Jesus wants all his children to be happy and restful and obedient. He promises that He will give us a special, easy, restful heart like He has. Nothing in the world can give you that kind of peaceful heart, but Jesus can. "Don't let your heart be upset; you don't have to be afraid" (John 14:27). Jesus tells us all this so that we can be full of His happiness and so that we can be glad (John 15:11).

Hard Times and a New Place to Live

One day David and Christy were at the kitchen table coloring while Mom was helping little Daniel play with some blocks. Dad was trying to fix a broken toy, and the radio was playing one of David's favorite songs. Soon the man on the radio began talking about an earthquake that had happened somewhere. Next he told about a robber who had broken into a house across town. The news went on with stories of fires and floods and car accidents.

David looked worried. "I know Jesus loves us. But why do so many bad things happen? Will it always be like this?"

"No," said Mom. "It will get worse."

The children looked up with wide eyes. "Why? Doesn't Jesus want us to be happy?"

"Of course, He does," Mom told them. "But, sadly, sin is getting worse all the time. People are getting worse. But God has promised to come and fix it all. Soon He'll take us home to His house to live with Him. Why don't you turn off the radio so we can read?"

Being Happy in Jesus

If you are selfishly looking to be happy and you don't want to obey God, you won't have a good time. When you think you're happy, you'll lose that happiness and be sad and lonely again—back and forth. But if you work for God, then you'll be happy. You won't have to be scared. You can know what to do and where to go. And even if you don't have a whole lot of happy times now, just remember that you'll be happier than you can imagine once you get to heaven.

But even now you can be happy because you have Jesus for your Friend. You can feel His love, and you'll always feel better because Jesus is near. Everything you do can make you better friends with Jesus and help you know Him better. You can be more sure than you ever were before. God has helped you until now, and He will help you until the end (1 Samuel 7:12).

Look at the things that God has already done for you and remember how He has saved you from Satan. Think about how kind God has been—how He has dried your tears when you cried and helped you feel so much better when you were hurting. He's helped you forget your worries and helped you not be afraid anymore. He's given you the things you needed and filled your life with good things. If you think about all these things, you can be strong to keep on living.

We know that we have hard times coming, but we can look at how well God has taken care of us before, and we can be sure that He will make us strong enough to meet all our problems (Deuteronomy 33:25). We'll never have problems too big to handle. Just keep doing the things you know you should do—and remember that whatever happens, God will make you strong enough to be the winner.

Before long, heaven's gates will be opened wide to let God's children come in. And then they will hear Jesus, their King, say, "Come in. My Father loves every one of you. It's time to live in the place that We've getting ready for you since the world was made!" (Matthew 25:34).

Then everyone who has been saved will go into the home that Jesus had made for them. They won't have to be around liars or evil people. They won't have to be around people with unclean hearts or people who don't believe in God. They will spend their time with other people who have won against Satan—people whom God has made perfect and lovely. Jesus will take away all the bad things. We won't be tempted or bothered anymore. We will be perfect. We will be wonderful and holy like Jesus! We won't have any sin in our hearts anymore, and we will be friends and workers with the angels!

When you think about all the wonderful things of heaven and know that you can have them, is anything more important to you than Jesus? Don't you want to get rid of everything that might take you away from Him? (Matthew 16:26).

Even if you are poor now, in Jesus you have everything that really matters. No one on earth can give you these treasures. When your heart has been saved and cleaned up from sin and you spend your time working for God, you'll be precious to Him. Jesus and the angels are so happy when one person is saved. They are so happy that everyone there sings the songs that only winners can sing.

A Real Book

Doesn't that sound wonderful?" Mom asked as she closed the book.

"Yes!" nodded Christy.

"I can't wait!" said David. "I want other people to come with me too." He jumped up from the table and came over to where Mom was sitting on the floor with Baby Daniel.

"Is that the end of our book? I've liked it a lot. I wish there were more and more to read." David looked at the book.

"Do you think we could let Laurie borrow it? Maybe Gordo, too, and some of our other friends? I think they'd like it."

Mom looked at Dad and smiled. "Actually, we just got good news. I sent the book to a book publisher, and soon it will be a real book—not just pages that we've put together into a book here."

Dad hugged Mom. "Aren't you proud of her?" he said to David and Christy. "Hasn't she done a good job?"

David and Christy started naming all their friends that they wanted to have a copy of the book.

Dad kissed Mom on the cheek. "Good job," he told her.

And Mom smiled.

If you and your child enjoyed this book, you'll want to read *Michael Asks Why* as well.

Michael Asks Why
Ellen G. White's Classic ***The Great Controversy*** Adapted for Children
Sally Pierson Dillon

To be of benefit, the readers (and listeners) need to have already heard the basic Bible stories. The purpose of this book is (a) to provide information for your children and answers to their questions, (b) to firmly ground them in their beliefs and the biblical basis for them, and (c) to help prepare them for Jesus' soon return and the investigative judgment—and to anticipate both with joy and confidence.

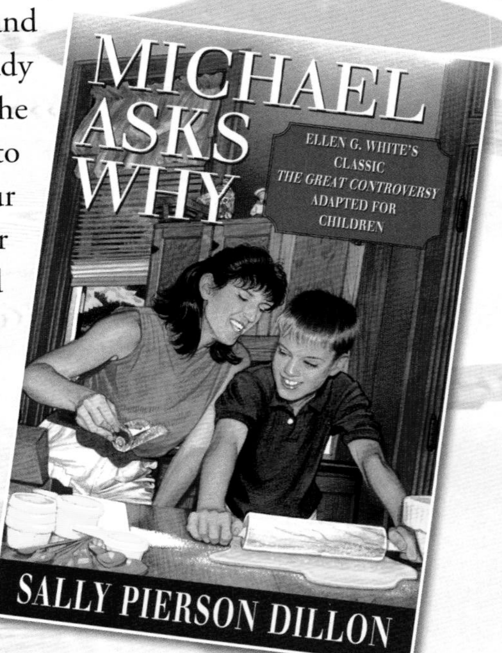

Beliefs/Kids 0-8163-1759-3

Three ways to order:

1 Local	Adventist Book Center®
2 Call	1-800-765-6955
3 Shop	AdventistBookCenter.com

©2009 Pacific Press® Publishing Association. 86013. Please contact your ABC for pricing in Canada.